Parents' Guide to Martial Arts

Parents' Guide to Martial Arts

by

Debra M. Fritsch and Ruth S. Hunter

Turtle Press   **Hartford, CT**

Parents' Guide to Martial Arts

To contact the author or order additional copies of this book:
Turtle Press
401 Silas Deane Hwy.
PO Box 290206
Wethersfield, CT 06129-0206
1-800-778-8785

Cover photos by Marc Yves Regis

Interior photos by Rob Ambrosius, David Comeau, Rick Klyssen, Ruth Hunter, Debbie Radloff, Marc Yves Regis, Wallace Roderick, Michael Stone, Barbara Talbot, William Therriault

ISBN 1-880336-22-7
First Edition
Library of Congress Number 98-209025

Cataloging in Publication data

Fritsch, Debra M.
    Parents' guide to martial arts / by Debra M. Fritsch and Ruth S. Hunter. -- 1st ed.
        p.   cm.
    Includes bibliographical references (p.   ) and index
    ISBN 1-880336-22-7
    1. Martial arts for children.   I. Hunter, Ruth S.   II. Title
GV1101.F75   1998
796.815--dc21   98-20902

Contents

Acknowledgments

Special thanks to the following people who have given so much of their time and energy to help us with this book:

Rob Ambrosius, Carole Basak, Jordan Blackmer, Lee Ann Blackmer, Marc Braiverman, Linda Clay, Tony Cogliandro, Tricia DeBlaey, Patrick Dinger, Penny Duggan, Heather Fritsch, James Fritsch, Kristin Fritsch, Stephen Gelin, Steve Godfriaux, Paul Harris, Floyd Jones, Fred Hammer, Marsha Hammer, Mark Heintzkill, Justin Hunter, Oriana Hunter, Theresa Hunter, William Hunter, Ralph Jensen, Paul Kegel, Tom Kegel, Cynthia Kim, Mary Alyce Lach, James Lee, Marilyn Lee, Micah O'Malley, Michelle Manke, Carol Margotto, Gary Margotto, Justin Margotto, Kiyomi Mimasu, Barbara Natelle, Charles Peterson, Wallace Roderick, Katy Rodon, Rob Serrano, Yoshifumi Shimada, Kazuko Stone, Matthew Stone, Michael Stone, Marta Stumbras, Barbara Talbot, Christine Talbot, Kim Talbot, Michelle Talbot, Kyoko Yoshimaru

To my family: Theresa for the uplifting, upside-down day; Justin and the fulfillment of his martial arts dreams; Oriana and her wonderful ability to read people; and to Bill for everything.

Ruth S. Hunter

Much love and gratitude to my family: Jim, Kristin, and Heather for their continued love and encouragement.

Debra L. Fritsch

Part 1

The Martial Arts
and Your Child

1

Why Martial Arts?

"Mom, Dad, I'd like to learn martial arts."

Welcome. You have just joined a growing number of children and their families across the nation who are interested in martial arts classes and what they teach. As a student, your child will participate in traditions that are thousands of years old but which have been modified to fit the needs of today's parent and child.

Martial arts lessons provide children with fun, exercise, discipline, self-respect, respect for others, self-control, and physical skills they can use their entire lives.

Since the early 1970s, the West has come to realize the martial arts are a means of self-defense, not simply methods of fighting. Children learn and practice awareness, quick thinking, ways to avoid situations as well as peaceful ways to control events.

The capacity of the martial arts to promote physical and mental health is widely appreciated and documented. Some of the positive changes in your child will be noticed immediately. Other changes will develop over time.

The following information will help you choose an instructor and school for your child which will enable both of you to have a wonderful and rewarding experience.

What Are the Physical Benefits?

It is fairly common to find that, historically, many martial artists took up the practice as sickly children. Both Master Gichin Funakoshi, shotokan karate's founder, and General Hong Hi Choi, a founder of taekwondo, had sickly childhoods.

Children studying the martial arts improve their general fitness including their reflexes, flexibility, coordination and agility. Exercise strengthens the muscles, builds strong bones, improves cardiovascular fitness, prevents heart disease and high blood pressure, and decreases depression. Physical fitness decreases stress, anxiety, and hostility, while it improves sleep habits, concentration, and energy levels.

Martial arts lessons also develop:

☆ Cardiovascular Fitness

Large portions of each martial art class are aerobic-type activities in which children must breathe properly, thus pushing oxygen to all parts of the body.

☆ Muscular Strength

Strength increases with consistent repetition of exercises and techniques. Martial artists develop strong biceps, forearms, thighs, calves, and abdominal muscles.

☆ Quick Reflexes

Quite a few of us have caught something just before it hits the ground and thanked our quick reflexes. And other times, unable to move, we have watched as the jar appeared to fall in slow motion before striking the floor and shattering into little pieces. While some people have naturally quick reflexes, most have to develop quick reactions.

A martial arts instructor credits his many years of training with saving his life in a motorcycle accident. His quick reflexes and repetitive training kicked in, and he tucked his head and rolled down the street, rather than slamming full-force onto the concrete.

Master Gichin Funakoshi credits quick reflexes learned from practicing the martial arts with saving him from drowning or at least a salty soaking when he was trying to cross a gangway from a bobbing ferryboat to a larger ship in rough seas. The sea grew wild just as he had one foot on the plank and one in the ferryboat and his hands hampered with heavy briefcases. Quickly, he switched a briefcase from one hand to the other, tossing the heavier briefcase further onto the gangway. The resulting momentum carried him to safety on the gangway.

Classes present many opportunities for children to improve their own reflexes as they react to their partner's moves or to the commands of the instructor.

☆Flexibility

"When my son was a baby, we watched in envy as he'd chew on his toes," a mother said. "He lost flexibility as he grew older, and when he started studying martial arts at age nine, he couldn't even touch his toes. A few years later, his father, who is 6'4", asked him how high he could kick. He placed the kick level with his dad's forehead."

As children grow, their bodies change and their legs often grow faster than their torsos. Normal play activities don't always keep them limber and flexible during this time of growth.

Martial arts classes include simple stretches and warm-ups which help keep children limber, and over a period of time, can recreate their early flexibility, adding to their enjoyment of everyday life. Increased flexibility enhances children's abilities to play, climb, jump, run, skate and walk without injury as well as enables them to perform high kicks and 360 degree turns.

☆ Coordination

Taking classes throughout childhood helps children to work through the awkward growth stages, to continually make adjustments based on their new size and improve their coordination and familiarity with their growing bodies.

Children learn at different rates of speed and have different learning styles. Learning to perform one punch correctly is quite an accomplishment in the early stages. As they progress, they are taught combinations of punches and kicks. With practice, they become quicker and more adept at moving their bodies naturally in a variety of ways.

What are the Mental Benefits?

Martial arts classes teach awareness, concentration, self-discipline, respect, and assertiveness. The by-products of these lessons are increased self-confidence and self-esteem. Children learn their capabilities and become aware of their ability to continually improve.

A general self-protection rule is knowing where you are and who is around you at all times. Awareness of your surroundings can protect you from an assailant or simply keep you from falling into a hole in the sidewalk.

Awareness is a skill that comes with practice. In class, children are taught to look at their partner's face while noticing the rest of their partner's body - the shoulders, eyes, hips, and legs. Will the partner do something more than just punch? At the same time, children are taught to notice where others are in the class. They learn to react to the immediate stimulus, and to be aware of and ready for unexpected developments.

This demands concentration. In addition to being aware of what is happening around them, children must focus on what they are doing so they can perform properly and with control. Through practice, they develop the abilities to concentrate and think clearly. Ultimately, learning to block outside worries, distractions, and problems in order to concentrate on one issue is a skill they can translate to other aspects of their lives.

Since physical activity releases hormones which decrease stress, children's moods improve with regular martial arts practice. A study performed in 1979 found that vigorous physical activity, such as the training received in martial arts classes, reduced anxiety. After a workout, students feel better and are able to deal appropriately with whatever feelings arose from the day's events.

Their self-esteem grows as they learn new skills and gain control over their bodies, accept and give critiques, and practice and perfect skills. They learn to accept and appreciate themselves for who they are.

Interacting with others of all ages helps them grow more self-confident and responsible and builds their self-esteem. As your child progresses through the ranks, he or she may soon be helping adults and be sought out as a source of information.

What Are the Social Benefits?

Martial arts schools provide many opportunities to make friends, including demonstrations, workshops, competitions, parties, and classes. Often, children from different elementary schools are members of the same martial arts school, giving them something to talk about when they run into each other outside of class.

During classes, children work by themselves within the larger group or are paired with others for partner exercises. This pairing rotates throughout the exercise so they are constantly faced with new people. Children interact with others while focusing on the instructor's directions and what they have to do - not on themselves. This makes martial arts classes especially helpful for shy children.

Children can succeed in the martial arts without being natural athletic stars. Even the most uncoordinated child will develop coordination with practice so that something which once required thought, becomes instinctive. It is often reassuring for children (and adults) to learn that black belts frequently struggled through the learning process. As their skills grow, children's confidence in what they can accomplish also grows. They are constantly working toward mastery of the art and having fun doing it.

Discipline and respect are stressed and differentiate the martial arts from school and recreational sports. Respect and appropriate behavior are integral parts of martial arts study.

Discipline refers to children's continued practice and training, to their ability to control their behavior in and out of class, and to their study of all aspects of the art.

Young martial artists learn ways to interact successfully with adults and upper belts, including calling an upper belt "Sir" or "Ma'am." Being respectful to adults and black belts does not imply children must believe everything that person says. It simply shows they acknowledge and respect the other person's expertise and knowledge.

Children also learn they are respected by how instructors and others in the class treat them. This ongoing interaction helps children develop confidence in dealing with others.

Another important aspect of martial arts study is self-control. Students must have self-control in order to learn, to keep from injuring themselves, to know when it is appropriate to use their skills, and to enable others to practice without fear of getting hurt. For example, practice helps them to estimate how far they must be from their partner in order to kick and punch without contact. They learn to control their actions and reactions.

How Does it Affect Children's Attitudes?

Children in the martial arts display confident attitudes. They have increased their self-esteem, physical abilities, and social skills. They worry less about possible dangers, real or imagined, than non-martial artists.

They realize they don't have to prove anything to anyone else, just to themselves. They are less likely to fight their way out of situations because of a need to prove themselves. They understand that they have more options.

What are the Educational Benefits?

The ancient roots of the martial arts form a base for today's most commonly studied versions. The uniforms are variations of common clothing worn thousands of years ago in Asia. Students often learn to respond to instructions and terminology in the art's native language. Many schools require a rudimentary knowledge of the country's history and culture from which their art developed; others require deeper knowledge.

As students gain this knowledge and grow in their skills and understanding, they are often asked to assist the instructor by helping lower ranking students. They are encouraged to learn how to work with others, no matter what their ages.

Everyone has the opportunity to workout with and help others before and after class. Sometimes during class, students will be asked to critique another person's movements or answer their questions. Students who take advantage of these opportunities learn more. While clarifying skills and knowledge for others, they do the same for themselves.

Studying martial arts offers children a whole new world of resources, beyond their academic classes, which will broaden their knowledge of other countries' cultures and histories. Martial arts catalogs, videos, books, school handouts and instruction are just a few resources available. Martial Arts provides a method through which children can begin to realize their global citizenship.

Potential Benefits of Martial Arts

Physical	Mental	Social
Cardiovascular Fitness	Awareness	Respect
Muscular Strength	Concentration	Self-Control
Quick Reflexes	Confidence	Interaction
Coordination	Responsibility	Leadership
Flexibility	Stress Relief	Assertiveness

What Kind of Self-Defense is Taught?

Self-defense is not simply reacting to attacks. Self-defense is also an attitude carried within oneself.

Often, parents try to shield children as much as possible from violence, including the evening news. Shielding children to a certain extent to create a secure childhood makes good sense—but only up to a point. Parents are not always with their children, especially as they grow older. This is when parents discover their protection is thin layered and does not provide the real protection children can get from knowledge.

Knowledge is protection. Information won't create paranoid children. Telling children about possible dangers and how to protect themselves is important to their safety--now and later as adults. Taught correctly, information won't frighten children, but will increase their self-confidence. A healthy respect for possible dangers differs from paranoia and an overall fear brought on by feeling defenseless.

Studies show that children who have developed self-defense skills are less anxious. They feel more self-confident and so are less likely to take risks. Children with self-defense skills are more socially intelligent, less naive, and have a higher level of self-esteem.

Learning how to carry themselves in order to avoid becoming victims and to be aware of their surroundings are basic self-defense skills which children can carry with them throughout their lives.

Martial arts based self-defense classes and workshops provide situational examples in safe, controlled atmospheres. Children practice different reactions and responses, learning to appreciate their rights and self-worth. They are encouraged to develop and follow their instincts.

Classes often include simple exercises such as asking students to close their eyes and describe the nearest exit or who the person is behind them. This helps them get into the habit of noticing their surroundings.

Repetition in classes is geared toward making movements and attitudes instinctual.   Children gain confidence and stand up for themselves. On a middle school camping trip, several boys picked up a young girl by her legs and arms to throw her into the water. It was a cold, rainy spring day; winter barely completed. She didn't want to go into the water. Using her martial arts skills and the self-esteem she'd developed, she kicked her foot toward the stomach of one boy. They recognized her determination not to be bullied and let her go.

As children continue martial arts practice, their self-esteem and self-confidence improve. They develop the confidence to speak up for their rights, to trust their gut instincts, and say "I don't have to accept this." They no longer feel defenseless.

Parents often teach children to respect their elders, that adults are always right. But, being older does not bestow upon a person an automatic niceness or rightness. Believing this can put children at a strong disadvantage. Since most child abuse originates from acquaintances, children must be taught at an early age what is private and what is appropriate behavior.

Self-defense begins with a strong sense of self-worth. Parents have the difficult task of teaching children to value the feelings of others while standing up for their own feelings and rights.

In addition to teaching physical skills, martial arts classes contribute to children's basic self-defenses skills by enhancing their self-esteem and self-confidence, helping them build a comfort level of interactions with adults, and teaching them to be aware of their surroundings and to trust their gut instincts.

Am I Encouraging a Mini-Rambo?

"Oh! That's much too violent," responded parents whose son told them his friend was taking the martial arts and he wanted to do so as well.

The parents were influenced by movies, combat martial arts, and stories of ninjas. They feared martial arts classes would make their son violent and aggressive.

The opposite is true. A study, "Aggressive Behavior as a Function of Taekwondo Ranking," tested the level of aggression in children ages six to eleven who were taking taekwondo. It found the longer the children took lessons, the less aggressive they became.

An earlier study by T.A. Nosanchuk of Carleton University examined students at a variety of martial arts schools. It found upper belt students had fewer aggression fantasies than lower ranked students who had not taken classes as long.

Far from creating mini-Rambos and mini-monsters, martial arts classes deal directly with many of the roots of aggressive behavior.

Over time, martial arts training actually decreases anxiety and aggression because children develop their senses of self and self-confidence. In *Psychology Today*, Michael Trulson points out that people who practice the martial arts develop a lower level of anxiety and are not as willing to take risks in order to prove themselves. They have increased senses of responsibility and self-esteem. Far from acting like bullies in order to feel in control, martial arts students understand they have control.

Children in the martial arts learn alternative ways of getting out of situations; that violence is not their only option. In one middle school, students picked on one particular boy. It became a "game" for them to body slam the boy into the lockers and to encourage others to do the same. After taking up martial arts, the boy learned to simply turn his body to avoid an attack and cause his attackers to slam into the lockers instead.

Trulson describes a study in which aggressive teenagers in trouble at school, with the law, and at home took traditional taekwondo classes. The youths radically changed their behavior, becoming more self-disciplined and respectful. Rather than creating mini-monsters, traditional martial arts training creates children with self-esteem, self-confidence and self-control.

What Are the Long-Term Benefits?

In Japan, intense martial arts training is basically for the young and the strong. Training can include students carrying other students on their backs while running up bleachers, or lying down and raising their legs off the floor while the teacher runs across their stomachs.

"It's rare to see someone in their 40s studying the martial arts in Asia with their child," Michael Stone said. Michael studied in Japan during his college years, becoming a sensei (teacher). While he now studies taekwondo with his son, he said few of his friends in Japan are still in the martial arts. "Their hearts are in it, but not their bodies."

In the United States, martial arts has become a recreational activity, with the training more well-rounded and accessible to people of all ages. It's not uncommon to find mothers and fathers taking classes with their children or to find a five-year old working out with a 65-year old.

In the 1970s, training in the United States was more intense than it is now and more injuries occurred. Today, many schools have no-contact or light-contact rules, and safety is a priority. In a well-run school, there are fewer injuries in a year than in a football or a basketball season.

Training builds upon basic movements. More difficult maneuvers are added as the student rises through the belt ranks. Each person can develop a strong base and practice perfecting that base.

Forty to 60-year olds might not be able to jump as high as they could in their teen years, but they can still work on their flexibility and on mastering techniques, take classes with their children, and have fun. They also have the advantage of life experiences which gives them an edge over younger students who might be more flexible but are not yet quite used to thinking on their feet.

For students interested in testing their skills, tournaments are offered locally, regionally, nationally and internationally. A student doesn't have to be a spry, athletic 20-year old male to compete. Each event is grouped according to age and rank, from the senior division to the very young, from black belts to white belts.

A recent national competition had rooms full of children competing in forms (prearranged routines) and free-sparring. Next to the musical forms, an older, blind man performed a weapons routine.

Since the study of the martial arts is more than a sport, it doesn't end with achieving a perfect kick or a black belt. One teenager reported thinking that getting her black belt would be an ending, a graduation point. "As I developed further in the arts, I recognized black belt as a beginning," she said. "There's so much more you can do."

Achieving the rank of black belt is an accomplishment. It designates a level of competence. However, it really is the beginning. Everything up to this point has been in preparation. In many traditional martial arts, the first three black belt degrees are novice levels. The next three degrees are intermediate and the final three are advanced. (In the United States, the levels have been modified in order to call a fifth degree black belt "Master Instructor.")

The study of the martial arts contains many elements, and people can spend hours reading, discussing, learning and growing. Martial arts becomes a part of them and who they are.

How Does Martial Arts Compare to Team Sports?

Martial arts is an individual activity, as opposed to a team sport. Whereas a child having a bad day in a team sport can depend on teammates to pick up the slack, children in the martial arts must rely on their own resources. How well they do in classes, promotions, or tournaments is up to them, no one else.

Tournaments provide opportunities for children to test their skills against themselves and against others. Since competition is viewed as one-on-one, the responsibility for doing well lands solely on the child, which means competitions can be intense. On the other hand, any child can compete. Competitions are not intended just for the star pupils, for the individuals who stand-out. Your child doesn't have to tryout and receive permission from a coach to compete or even to participate in the activity. Martial arts tournaments offer more age and skill levels than most other sports, and anyone who wants to compete with others of the same age and skill level can do so.

Some competitions now offer optional "Physically Challenged" divisions for children and adults. Although it states "Physically Challenged" as the title, the division is not limited to people in wheelchairs or braces, but is open to children and adults with a wide variety of disabilities such as autism, blindness, and Down Syndrome.

After each tournament event, each competitor can come away knowing how they would like to improve their performance. Learning to take responsibility for their performance, rather than blaming the judges or another factor is a healthy sign of maturity.

Competitions are not for everyone. Many martial artists feel the competitive nature of tournaments has little to do with the serious practice of martial arts and shun them completely. It is up to you and your child to decide whether or not to enter competitions.

Most children can learn martial arts skills and participate in group building activities in which their individuality shines. They have a talent they can perform in front of peers or as part of school demonstrations.

How well or fast your child advances in the martial arts ranks is up to him or her. Even young children learn that if they desire to do well, they must back up the desire with hard work and practice. This requires personal dedication and is a good lesson to learn; one that will last their entire lives.

How Does it Relate to Daily Life?

☆ Common Sense

A high school freshman described taking her five-year old brother to the movies. "Someone started shooting," she said. "I was trying to get out of there, and he wanted to stand on the seat and see what was happening."

Rarely is someone born with an overabundance of common sense. Common sense or instincts are based on what people have heard from others or experienced themselves. For instance, young children will roll off the sofa's edge because they don't realize that edges are dangerous. They learn it's dangerous either because they listen to the advice of their parents or because they have fallen off.

Martial arts classes provide a safe atmosphere in which children can practice safety skills and build a base of self-defense knowledge. Self-defense classes can accurately depict scenes in which children might find themselves. Children can learn to assess situations, even before there is a hint of trouble.

Students learn to rely on their instincts. A second degree black belt leaving class by herself one night noticed a hunched over man walking up an adjoining street. Then she noticed he was quickly covering ground—too fast for an elderly person. She increased her pace. When the man cut across the parking lot towards her, she was already unlocking her car. She threw in her equipment, entered, locked and started the car—a combination she had practiced, and immediately drove off. Her training would have helped her confront the man if necessary, but more appropriately, it allowed her to notice and judge the man's actions, think calmly and remove herself from a possible situation.

Given different situations, children can learn and practice many physical and verbal responses which are geared to their age and ability levels. Best of all, their logical thinking skills and their awareness of their surroundings are increased.

☆ Emotional Maturity

On a stairway at a high school, one boy purposefully bumped into the boy above him on the stairs and raised his fists. "Come on," the boy said, "I want to fight."

Unknown to him, the boy he had challenged was a second degree black belt. The black belt looked at the boy's upraised arms and knew exactly how easy it would be to take him down. Instead, he said, "I don't feel like getting expelled today," and walked away.

Many studies show the amount of self-control and discipline exhibited by students relates directly to how long they've studied the martial arts.

In addition to learning how to use skills, children learn when to use their skills. They learn to judge what are the most appropriate actions in different situations, and they can develop an inner security which helps them walk away from situations instead of being manipulated into proving themselves.

☆ Concentration

Children have to put the day's worries behind them when they enter the martial arts school. In spite of what happened in school or at home, their responsibility is to focus on class activities. They practice this type of focus with each class exercise. Even though they are aware of others in the class, they concentrate on the movements they are practicing and on the instructor.

This skill can be used in other aspects of their lives, helping them concentrate on current issues and not let other events affect their general behavior. It is a skill that once internalized will help them as they become older and enter the working world.

☆ Leadership Growth

As students continue to advance, they are given many chances to grow as leaders.

These opportunities start in class when they are partnered with other students, regardless of age or rank. All students ask their partners questions and listen to the answers. They critically evaluate their partner's skills and make suggestions to improve them.

Youngsters' leadership potential becomes formalized when they become assistants and act as an extension of the teacher, helping to reach all students in the class.

Outside of class, the ability to observe, critique, and suggest solutions translate into leadership abilities and form a strong basis for a successful life.

When is Martial Arts Not a Good Idea?

While for a vast majority of students, martial arts is a uniformly positive experience, this is not true for all. Parents and instructors should evaluate certain young people very carefully before allowing them to participate in the martial arts.

These include children who have exhibited explosive, aggressive outbursts; histories of alcohol or other drug abuse; violent tendencies; or children whose only motivation is to "kick someone's butt." Some studies have indicated that martial arts can be "therapeutic," but this only works if training is part of an overall long-term treatment plan, not the plan itself.

Children, whose parents are forcing them to take martial arts to cure perceived problems of aggression, timidity, or lack of self-esteem, may also not be suitable candidates. The desire to learn the martial arts and overcome their problems must also come from the children.

Martial arts are systems of physical and mental training which stress long-term, lifelong learning. People of any age seeking short-term, quick fix solutions will be disappointed and frustrated.

Real Life Profile

"I went to Asia because of the martial arts, and it has affected every aspect of my life." - Michael Stone

Michael and Matthew Stone

Son's Interest Renews Father's Interest

When Michael Stone was 12, he began studying the martial arts with an uncle, Tom Hettrick, who had served in Vietnam and had lived in Japan. Michael studied awhile in Oklahoma when his family moved there, but took a few years off when his family returned to Wisconsin.

When it came time to select a college, he decided to travel to Japan, immerse himself in the culture, and pursue martial arts study. "From 1980 to 1983, there were very few Americans studying in Japan," Michael said. "I was alone pretty much, certainly within the martial arts."

In addition to attending college classes in Tokyo, Michael studied shorinji kempo and iaido (Japanese sword) and received Zen training as part of his iaido training.

His iaido teacher, Shigezou Kosaka Sensei, was 81 years old and a ninth degree black belt in iaido and fourth degree black belt in kendo. "Rumor was that his father was one of the last samurai, so Kosaka Sensei was of Samurai stock. But I can't confirm the rumor," Michael said.

"We felt more than respect and love for our sensei," Michael said. "Although he was old, he came to teach us in winter, walking through the snow. He would go through the movements so patiently and slowly for us."

One time, Kosaka Sensei forgot to tell the students they could leave before he went home. Michael and his colleagues stayed in their positions on the floor. "No one wanted him to return and find out we were gone," Michael said. Finally, Kosaka Sensei remembered and returned by bus to the studio to release the class.

Kosaka Sensei's final act was to teach his students one more iaido class. "He went home and died two hours later," Michael said.

Michael and his wife gave their oldest son, Michael, the middle name of Shigetake, Shige after the sword teacher and Take after his grandfather in Japan.

Michael lived in a private boarding house, Wakei Juku, on grounds once owned by a wealthy samurai. "It was an old building turned into dormitories, but it had a dojo," Michael said.

Michael practiced barefoot for hours each day on the wooden floors of the unheated dojo. "It was freezing in winter," he said. "And hot in the summer."

He studied shorinji kempo and iaido two to three hours daily, with a more intensive workout of six to eight hours on Saturday and Sunday. He would attend college classes, run to his shorinji kempo lessons and then back to the dormitory for sword lessons.

There was no dojo in which to study kempo, so the students studied outside on asphalt in all seasons from sunny weather to rain and snow. Before the start of each class, they ran barefoot on the Tokyo streets.

"At first," Michael said. "I had tender feet. I was six feet tall, and a shorter senpai, a senior club mate, came up behind me and grabbed both me and another person and pushed us along."

In classes held in the United States, Michael notices people work out with varying degrees of effort. "In Japan, everyone worked equally as hard. Not just one person would have to do push-ups as punishment; they all would have to do push-ups. There was tremendous pressure to keep up with the group. If anyone slacked, the seniors would be angry, and they would express their anger with their eyes. It was important that we progressed together as a group."

To keep everyone together, Michael explained the senior members practiced outside of class with individuals until their skills matched the group.

He, like the others in his class, reached a point where he could communicate without speaking. "We knew each other well and worked as a unit," Michael said. "We are really heavy on verbal communication in the States. We don't want to listen to our gut feelings."

When it was time to test for his black belt, Michael had to choose whether to undergo the three-week long test or stay in college. He chose to test and went to Shikoku Island, where the headquarters for shorinji kempo and a practice ground are located.

Michael became a sensei and later taught at Gashuku, a martial arts summer training camp in Nikko. When he returned to college, Michael needed a tutor to help him catch up on his studies. He asked Kazuko, a young woman who sat next to him in class. She agreed. They later married in the States.

He returned to the United States when he was 23 and found it hard to adjust, discovering his philosophy of life was much different from his contemporaries.

Michael became involved in work and family. For 12 years, he didn't do martial arts, becoming "rusty." Then his son, Matthew, who was around six-years old at the time, asked Michael to teach him the martial arts.

"We went into the backyard, and I found out that I couldn't kick to head level," Michael said. "I'd never lost a tournament in Japan. You don't think it's gone away, but with marriage and kids, years passed. Matthew got me back into it."

On weekends, they worked out in the backyard. Michael discovered the concepts of Asian training were too radical for a six-year old so he interviewed various martial arts instructors until he found one. At first, the differences in the teaching styles between classes in Japan and classes in the United States, bothered him. He thought classes were too easy and informal; classes looked like playing and not training.

But he stayed in the classes for Matthew's sake and because he knew he didn't have the self-discipline to work out by himself everyday.

Matthew thinks having his father in class is better than just studying by himself. "Dad could tell me if I was real serious. I could work with him after class," Matthew said.

Michael enjoys the opportunity. "It's really nice. As a young man, I'd think about family life and having a son to teach martial arts to and then there you are—a son, you're teaching him martial arts and he enjoys it, and he's good at it too.

"Now I'm glad I stayed. These classes have given me a different perspective on the martial arts. It becomes a lifelong activity, accessible to more people, to older people."

He has had instructors from Asia tell him that the United States is keeping the study of the martial arts alive. "They said: 'You're going to teach our grandchildren, because it's dying here.'"

Michael's job involves much international travel. He studies taekwondo in Korea, tai chi ch'uan and kung-fu in China and silat fighting in Indonesia.

He has used the arts to defend himself. "It sure helped in Philippines when I had no chance to run. I was glad to have the skill."

And he uses the arts to communicate. "When I travel to China, I can relate to them through the martial arts. I can compare my company's idea to tai chi—a flexible motion. I tell them my competitor is like karate—a really hard art.

"More than tennis and regular sports, martial arts becomes a part of your life," Michael said. "It changes the way you think, especially for me. My mentors were all martial artists. But if Matt was not in it now, I wouldn't have returned to it."

2

Are Martial Arts Right for my Child?

Experts have established broad guidelines of what can be expected physically and mentally from children at various ages. These guidelines are averages since children develop at differing rates. Expecting too much or too little can compromise children's developing self-images.

In the martial arts, children can work to the best of their abilities and at their own pace. They aren't expected to be a certain height or weight; they can succeed by working with and improving the abilities they were born with.

Boys do not automatically do better than girls. Recent research has shown girls and boys involved in similar activities before puberty develop similar physical skills and abilities.

After the onset of puberty, most boys develop bulkier body frames and gain weight. By age fourteen, their interest in athletics has grown, and they admire others with good athletic abilities. They enjoy pitting their athletic abilities against their peers.

By the time girls reach fourteen, their interest in sports often depends on the availability of sports for females in their area and how socially acceptable these sports are to their families and cultures.

What Should I Expect for My Child's Age Level?

Your child is an individual who may or may not be physically advanced and emotionally in line with his or her peers. Each child grows and matures at different rates.

Most children are ready to start simple martial arts skills between ages four and five. Some signs of readiness include following directions, spatial awareness, listening skills, and self-control (i.e., not hitting others).

In general terms, young children, ages four to eight, are often more concerned with the process of learning than with mastering skills.

Those aged nine to twelve are often skill hungry. They're continually seeking new skills and not particularly interested in perfecting old skills.

As children enter the teen years, they are more likely to specialize in one or two sports. They have less time to try everything and are more concerned with making serious, long-term commitments. They often excel.

For example, Kuk Hyun Chung began studying taekwondo in his late teens and has made the *Guinness Book of Sports Records*—a number of times. He has won the most World Championship titles by a single person (1982, 1983, 1985, 1987). In 1984 and 1985, he won the Athlete's Award for outstanding competition performance, and he won the gold medal in taekwondo in the 1988 Summer Olympics. He is undefeated in international competition.

Below are some insights as to what you might reasonably expect of your child at each age level.

☆ Three to Four Years

"For the most part, children ages three to four-years old haven't developed as many of their physical capabilities as older children," a Montessori teacher said. "Their large and small motor skills are in the process of developing. Three-year olds still have the toddler gait and their muscle coordination is just beginning."

Ages three and four are good times to help children perfect their balance. One exercise involves placing bean bags on children's heads and shoulders while they walk on a line. "It develops their sense of inner control and balance," the Montessori teacher said.

More coordinated than they were at three, four-year olds are exuberant and have more control over their physical abilities. Four-year olds like lots of activity and aren't concerned with reaching perfection. They want to try new things, but trying something once may be enough for them.

Girls may become skilled with complicated movements earlier than boys. "Four-year old girls are more focused physically," an early childhood teacher said. "They are better at skipping, while boys are better at running."

At four-years old, children begin playing in groups. They are a little more confident when answering out loud simple questions such as "Did you have fun?"

☆ Five Years

Coordination continues to improve in five-year olds. They have more command over their movements and display more large muscle control than small muscle control.

They are fairly good judges of their own abilities and prefer looking positively at things. They tend to stay with the activities they are sure they can accomplish and work from there to build on their own successes.

Five-year olds have learned to function in large groups. They try hard to do the right things, and most of the time, they will be able to control themselves and follow the school's rules.

☆ Six Years

Energetic six-year olds have a hard time standing still. With all of this energy, their muscle control lessens when they tire.

Six-year olds are not yet logical thinkers. Their understanding of appearance and reality is not fully formed. They may assume someone is good at martial arts because they are who they are, not because they have practiced for many years.

The line between reality and fantasy is thin, and they give objects a state of consciousness. If they miss a target when practicing kicks, they may think the target moved to avoid being kicked.

They generally can not reverse an idea. If asked to take three steps to the front and punch and then move three steps to the rear and punch, they may not understand the only change in the two commands is direction.

Their attention spans aren't long, and they may be easily distracted, however, they like attention and praise from their teachers and don't like being corrected.

☆ Seven Years

Seven-year olds are more selective in picking their activities and in how much energy they exert to complete them. They are easily distracted and may need reminding to finish a task.

While their performance levels remain steady, the goals they set for themselves may be too ambitious for their abilities. They can be too critical of themselves, worry about everything and quit when things get too hard. They might have trouble accepting praise. They want to be part of the group and don't like being singled out for compliments or criticism.

To complete a task, they will have to follow the same steps each time. A child who learns a martial arts form while facing the front of the room, may not be able to turn to the back of the room and repeat the same form.

☆Eight Years

Eight-year olds are energetic and fast with good eye and hand coordination. They have large muscle control and show marked improvement in the quickness and fluidity of their small muscles. However, their attention easily shifts to whatever is happening in their peripheral vision which can be confusing, especially during sparring bouts.

Eight-year olds recognize different people have different perspectives, and they understand the relationship between cause and effect. They are competitive and can lose without taking it too personally. The concept of time begins to make sense to them, and they can be responsible for being on time.

They love new and more complex tasks and have begun to think logically and abstractly, making this a good time to take on more advanced martial arts concepts. They understand performing a series of movements and repeating them on the other side.

The wild energy of an eight-year old responds well to guidance. They obey best if corrections are given as amiable reminders or as secret codes, often arranged in advance. Instead of saying "Bobby, don't drop your fists," the instructor can simply say, "Fists."

☆ Nine Years

While not as energetic as eight-year olds, nine-year olds play very hard and quite possibly to the point of exhaustion. Their eyes and hands work well together, and their motor skills have reached a new level. They enjoy showing off their skills in demonstrations and testing their competence in control and timing through competition.

They expect discipline to be fair and will accept it if it is. They demand and appreciate fair evaluations from others and themselves.

Nine-year olds are self-motivated and can finish tasks without being continually reminded of goals. They can be interrupted and corrected midway through a movement and then go on to finish the movement. They are willing to do something over and over again to perfect it. This is a trait that will increase the child's chances of improvement markedly over younger, less patient children.

Always willing to try new things, the nine-year old wants more information before beginning something. Strong wills and desperate desires for success make failures tough to handle, and they may offer excuses to cover their failures.

☆ Ten Years

Ten-year olds prefer activities which use their large motor skills and aren't overly vigorous. Most ten-year old students are open to being taught and supervised and will follow rules. They can have quick tempers.

Though their memorization skills have improved, they still don't apply deep meaning to the information. Competitions are still fun, but they may have a problem with winning, since they now realize other children are losing. Ten-year olds are still sensitive to issues of fairness. In times of struggle, they take on challenges squarely and with a certain air of grace.

☆ Eleven Years

Eleven-year olds thinking is more complex, and they consider more possibilities when developing plans to solve problems.

This is an age of highly conflictive and combative behavior. They either love or hate things; there's very little middle ground. Conflict seems to follow them, and while they feel they can do nothing right, they need to prove themselves right. Eleven-year olds are competitive but can have short attention spans.

Getting the eleven-year old to do assigned tasks may be a challenge. Students respond well to instructors and adults other than their parents. At this age, martial arts classes can provide guidance for a child who is difficult to manage at home.

☆ Twelve Years

Twelve-year olds are more self-confident and comfortable expressing their opinions. Their energy levels fluctuate between periods of hyperactivity and doing nothing. If they are extremely interested and committed to a project, their energy levels are high.

They can handle more responsibility and embrace the advancement toward adulthood. It is often around this age that children are encouraged to join an adult class and learn more challenging skills.

☆ Thirteen Years

Despite being withdrawn, thirteen-year olds have high energy levels. They like challenging projects which they can work on at their own pace. The individual nature of martial arts can provide a welcome opportunity for this type of mental stimulation. They are suddenly aware of their growing intellectual skills.

Fairness still ranks high in the thirteen-year olds' reasoning. While they try to do right, they may still prefer to find fault rather than take responsibility.

☆ Fourteen Years

Although they recognize their own faults, fourteen-year olds they may be reluctant to correct them. They feel they know how to control themselves and do not like to be corrected.

Their problem solving skills are low. They can take in too much information, disregard none of it and become indecisive as a result. In class, teenagers are ready for anything. Their light attitudes can make classes lots of fun.

Students want to perform well and like to compete in areas in which they excel. But because teen activities are so diverse, they may not put in the work needed to accomplish their goals.

When Should a Child Take Up Martial Arts?

When your child expresses an interest in learning the martial arts, find out where this idea came from. If it is your child's idea, the chances for success are better than if he or she is reacting to outside pressure from parents, friends, or siblings.

Siblings who are close in age often join at the same time and take classes together. They have to understand they are not competing against each other, but are learning at their own pace. There really is not any room or need for sibling rivalry. Instructors and parents can help create a non-competitive attitude by treating each child's abilities and successes separately.

When to start children in the martial arts is a decision made after considering their personalities and reasons for joining as well as their ages.

Some families find children begin one by one as they develop an interest Other families wait until their children become old enough to take classes together. Often, a younger sibling starts after spending a few years watching classes from the waiting room.

If one child is more athletic, he or she will learn more quickly. But this does not mean only athletic children will succeed in the martial arts.

Many times, those who are the least athletic will stay in the martial arts longer and advance further, because they work harder. They are used to not being recognized as an athletic star right away. An exciting time for them and a great incentive is when they finally realize how far they have advanced compared to where they were in the beginning. They have succeeded at a physically demanding activity.

Natural athletes sometimes become bored and quit when they feel they have achieved a certain level of expertise. Injuries sustained in other sports can affect the natural athlete's martial arts career. Two sisters, one athletic and one scholastic, joined at the same time. Because of cheerleading injuries, the more athletic one stopped taking lessons while the other achieved her black belt.

What Can I Expect My Child to Get Out of Martial Arts?

Parents often have specific reasons for enrolling their children in the martial arts. Children have their own expectations.

Martial arts are often seen as a means to teach self-defense or a way to learn assertiveness. One father signed his daughter up for martial arts lessons because she was being picked on in school.

"I knew it would give her more confidence," he said. "Not to beat someone else up, but if someone threatened her, she could do something."

Parents who studied the martial arts in their youth may have fond memories of classes and the confidence they gained. They want their children to share in the same experiences.

Other parents are concerned their children aren't tough enough. A father, who had learned martial arts skills while serving in the army, enrolled his four-year old son in weekend classes. He expressed concern that his son was too soft and uncoordinated. Fearing this behavior was permanent, he wanted his son to "toughen up."

In spite of popularly held beliefs, many boys aren't born "rough and tumble." This comes with age. As boys mature, their testosterone levels rise and so does their need to compete.

One child, at age nine, worried about having to leave home when he grew up. At times, he hugged his mother after class. A few years later, the boy achieved his black belt. Later, he taught advanced classes, concentrating on physical as well as mental aspects of the martial arts. Students of all ages looked forward to his workouts. Outside of class, he sparred others from his school as well as from other schools. By the time he was 17, the young man was more than ready to blast full-force into responsible adulthood.

Martial arts alone will not toughen children. It can teach them to be aware, to think, and to react appropriately. It provides children with personal space to learn about themselves and their abilities, and to practice social and coping skills.

3

Which Martial Art is the Right One?

The martial arts are systems of fighting skills which developed over thousands of years. Long before the invention of weapons, prehistoric humans used their hands and feet to defend themselves. You will find each martial art and its philosophy is closely related to the country from which it evolved.

It was in Asia that hand and foot fighting techniques developed into the martial arts as we know them today. One of the more popular stories tells how Bodhidharma brought the martial arts from India to the Shaolin Temple in China. He had discovered the monks at the temple lacked the stamina necessary to concentrate long hours in prayer. Studying the martial arts increased their stamina.

Monks skilled in various styles of martial arts traveled throughout Asia, teaching their skills and hiring out as warriors.

Believing strongly that true warriors were more than fighting machines, ancient samurai warriors studied tea ceremonies, art, religion, and philosophy to enhance their social and intellectual skills.

While highly developed in Asia, the martial arts also appeared in other parts of the world. Over 2,000 years ago, the Romans and Greeks broke stones, boards, and bricks to demonstrate their strength and abilities. For practice, they shadowboxed and performed forms, a series of movements which they had created from their favorite fighting techniques. Roman and Greek myths describe some of the same fighting techniques found in Asia, and sculptures of ancient Roman warriors depict classic empty-hand fighting.

Throughout both Asian and European history, soldiers and warriors have yelled before battles. Similarly the kihap used by martial artists sounds like a loud shout and is used to scare opponents, to help the martial artist focus and to tighten muscles in the body.

As wars broke out in the late 1800s and early 1900s, European soldiers brought back stories of the empty-hand fighting they had faced in Asia. It was the amazing control martial artists had over their bodies, their speed, their awareness, and quick thinking which impressed soldiers. This led to martial arts demonstrations on many military bases.

In the movie, *Indiana Jones and the Raiders of the Lost Ark*, Jones faces an opponent skilled in swordsmanship. Jones shoots him. This is a condensed view of what happened to the martial arts warrior. As firearms became more sophisticated, ancient weapons fell out of daily use. Many of the weapons forms taught today are ceremonial, such as iaido, the art of the Japanese sword.

The spread of the martial arts to the United States occurred as far back as 1848 during the Gold Rush when Chinese laborers, secretly skilled in kung-fu, were imported to work in the mines. Judo was introduced in 1902 and demonstrated at the White House in 1903. The existence of the martial arts reached a large number of Westerners with the 1921 movie, *Outside Woman*.

As martial arts expanded throughout the world, the various styles adapted techniques from each other and continued to evolve, developing new styles. In the United States, the arts are mostly recreational, a popular sport and exercise which even children can learn and enjoy.

What Is a Martial Arts "Style"?

Martial arts styles can be described as hard or soft, linear or circular, external or internal. Soft styles are circular in motion, deflecting attacks with parries and throws, and using the opponent's strength against him. Soft styles are referred to as internal. Mediation and philosophy are found more often in soft, internal styles. Hard styles, referred to as external, contain more linear movements such as kicks and punches and rely more on strength and firmness to stop an attack. Competition and combat are stressed in the hard or external styles. Many of today's martial arts such as taekwondo and shotokan karate contain elements of both styles.

Are Martial Arts Skills Shown in Movies the Same as Those Taught in Schools?

"When do we learn the flying kick?" asked an eight-year old during his first summer weekend class. At this point, the boy had no idea how to correctly make a fist.

He had watched martial arts moves on TV shows and movies where the heroes and heroines kick, punch and somersault over sixteen villains, all while never getting hurt.

In *Lethal Weapon II*, Mel Gibson may start the back spinning kick, but a stuntman accomplished in the martial arts, completes it. Bruce Lee, in his role in the TV series, *The Green Hornet*, actually had to slow down his moves because he was too fast for the camera.

Real fights are over quickly. But a quick fight wouldn't create the excitement and tension which movies want to instill in viewers. Long fight scenes with fast paced techniques and intricate movements are elaborately choreographed by experts and are smoothly fought by actors and stunt people working together. Intricate movements and smooth, flowing techniques do not exist in real life fights.

What Are Some Styles of Martial Arts?

In addition to the hundreds of martial arts styles which originated in Asia, are those which originated in Europe and the Americas. If you live in a large city, you may have many styles to choose from, while if you live in a smaller town, you may be able to choose from only one or two.

Style can be important (i.e., a combative style versus an internal style, or a throwing style versus a kicking style), but the school's philosophy and instructor's ability are often more important to your child's enjoyment of and long-term commitment to the martial arts.

The following section is an abbreviated, general information list of martial arts styles. In it, you'll find descriptions of common styles that may be taught in your area as well as descriptions of familiar styles which are not commonly taught today, and styles which are based on various weapons. You can use this information to help identify a martial arts style that is right for your child.

If you find that a school in your area teaches an art form not listed here, ask the instructor for some literature about the background of the art or do your own research at the library or over the internet. If you cannot find any information about the art, it may be an eclectic art developed by the instructor or by his or her teacher. In this case, read over the section beginning on page 54 about the pros and cons of learning a eclectic art.

☯ Aikido

Definition: The Japanese characters for aikido mean harmony, energy, and the way. Aikido is a soft style, unarmed martial art which moves with the flow of force rather than against it. The aikido practitioner uses the attacker's forward momentum against him by making the attacker overextend himself and lose balance. Most movements are circular.

Techniques include throws and joint locks. Understanding leverage, redirection of force and timing are essential aspects of the training. Formal katas (prearranged routines) teach the proper use of the jo (short staff), one of the more commonly taught weapons in aikido.

Origin: Japan

History: Aikido was developed by Morihei Ueshiba in 1942 after he studied hundreds of martial arts. Ueshiba wanted to develop a system which would enable the martial artist to grow physically (externally) and mentally (internally), allowing the practitioner to remain in harmony with the attacker and with nature. Aikido traces back through daito-ryu aiki-jutsu which grew out of kenjutsu (sword art).

Variations and Substyles: Aikido for competition: Tomiki aikido (ninin-dori, radori kyochi, tanto randori) and yoshin aikido.

☯ Bojutsu

Definition: Bojutsu is a combat, self-defense style which uses a five to six-foot long wooden bo, otherwise known as a staff. Skill with the bo is developed by practicing kata, a formalized set of movements. Bojutsu was traditionally very effective against the sword.

Origin: Japan

History: The Japanese modified Chinese techniques and created new ones. Izasha Inenao is credited with founding the katori shinto-ryu style of this martial art, upon which all Japanese jojutsu (stick) systems are based. The original weapons were a combination of wood and iron. Because wooden versions were safer for practice, several weapons arts evolved including rokushaku-bo and jodo. The bokken (a wooden sword) was used in training by all Japanese warriors.

Variations and Substyles: Over 316 in Japan.

☯ Hapkido

Definition: Hapkido, meaning "way of harmony," is practiced as a form of self-defense and combines elements of aiki-jutsu, taekyon and hwarang-do.

Origin: Korea

History: The founder, Yong Shul Choi, studied daito-ryu aiki-jutsu in Japan. He helped form the Korean Kido Association in the 1960s. Some of his students left and founded the Korean Hapkido Association.

☯ Iaido

Definition: Iaido is the art of drawing the Japanese samurai sword; a modern form of the samurai practice of iaijutsu. As iaido, it relies deeply on spiritual or religious dimensions. The practitioner performs the art in four stages; drawing the sword, striking, cleaning of the blade and returning the sword into the scabbard. The movements are practiced in kata (forms) with a few sparring forms such as three-step sparring. Modern iaido falls under the All-Japan Kendo Federation.

Origin: Japan

Variations and Substyles: Gunto soho and omori-ryu iai.

☯ Jeet Kune Do

Definition: Jeet kune do draws from many arts. It emphasizes using appropriate and effective techniques in real life situations, rather than relying on stylized, rigid reactions. The goal is to develop a personal understanding of oneself.

Origin: U.S.A.

History: Bruce Lee created this art in 1967 while looking for a style that stayed fluid and adapted to real-life situations. Even his teaching style differed from other arts. He taught a few students at a time so he could pay stricter attention to the individual habits of each student.

☯ Jojutsu

Definition: The art was developed to teach the use of a 4'2" stick called a jo. Use of the jo is practiced against the bokken (wooden sword) in katas (forms). The practitioner builds upon twelve basic techniques, ultimately learning more than 70 advanced techniques.

Techniques include strikes, blocks, parries, counters, pressure points, and evasive body moves.

Origin: Japan

History: About 400 years ago, Muso Gunnosuke founded jojutsu after he was defeated by the famous swordsman Miyamoto Musashi in a battle with wooden swords. Using jojutsu, he later defeated Miyamoto Musashi.

Variations and Substyles: Jodo is an offshoot of jojutsu. In the 1950s, practice of the art was resumed after being banned after World War II. The student of jodo usually goes on to study additional weapons and martial arts. Keibo soho is a variation developed for the police.

☯ Judo

Definition: Judo means the gentle way and is considered both a martial art and a sport. It follows strict rules which makes it a popular international sport. The student studies how to get the maximum benefit from the least amount of action. The student wins by yielding to the opponent and using the opponent's strength against him. Techniques such as falls, grips, sweeps and throws, and restraints are combined with a strong understanding of leverage.

Origin: Japan

History: Founded by Jigoro Kano in 1882 after extensive study of various forms of jujutsu. Judo, governed by the International Judo Federation, was officially accepted by the Olympics as a competitive sport for men in 1964 and for women in 1992.

☯ Jujutsu (Jujitsu)

Definition: Jujutsu is an unarmed, grappling art as well as a weapons art designed to be effective in close range combat. Over the years, jujutsu, has become a term often been used to cover a broad range of fighting methods.

Origin: Japan

History: Jujutsu was used widely when hand-to-hand combat was common. It declined with the invention of modern weapons.

Variations and Substyles: Many variations developed over the years with the most influential being tenjin shinyo-ryu, sekiguchi ryu, kito ryu, takenouchi ryu, sousuishitsu ryu. A recent offshoot is the development of Brazilian jujitsu, made popular in "no-holds-barred" competitions.

☯ Karate

Definition: Karate, a hard style art designed for self-defense, teaches strikes and blows performed with hands and feet aimed at specific areas of the body. The term "karate" means empty hand. Techniques are grounded in proper stances, breathing, speed and hip flexibility.

Teachers and students follow traditional rules which decree how they treat one another. Colored belts designate the ranks beneath black. Karate principles apply to learning and achieving standing within the art and are meant to be used as a way of life. (Note: Karate is often used as a generic term to describe all martial arts.)

Origin: China, India, Okinawa

History: Modern karate was founded by Gichin Funakoshi in the early twentieth century. The earliest forms of the ancient art can be traced to China, India, and Okinawa.

Major Variations:

☯ Okinawan Kempo
Founded in the early 1900s by Shigeru Nakimura and Zenryoku Shimabuku, Okinawan kempo is rooted in Chinese kempo. The style encourages full-contact sparring to help keep up the art's original combat effectiveness.

☯ Shito-Ryu
In 1930, Kenwa Mabuni founded this hard style karate which includes soft style techniques and equally emphasizes katas, sparring, and basics.

☯ Shorinji Kempo
An art originally taught only to Buddhist monks. Bodhidharma taught kempo at the Shaolin Temple and shorinji means Shaolin. Meditation and action are equally emphasized in training. Doshin So is credited with the revisions that created modern day shorinji kempo.

☯ Shotokan
Gichin Funakoshi founded Japanese shotokan in 1917, combining two Okinawan martial arts to form karate-do. Most techniques are linear. In 1949, various clubs and dojos organized into the Japan Karate Association.

☯ Kenjutsu (Kendo)

Definition: Kenjutsu is an ancient sword art used by the samurai.

Origin: Japan

History: The art was taught in secret by the master to the students. They then learned other fencing arts to understand how to defend against them. Strict codes defining proper targets for warriors were defined, but the codes were not always followed.

Variations and Substyles: The most popular subdivision is kendo which began over 1,500 years ago. Students wear samurai clothing: divided skirt (hakama), apron and jacket and compete with bokken (wooden sword). Other major substyles of this art form include jigen ryu, shingen-ryu, kum do, and nihon kendo kata.

☯ Kenpo (American Kenpo)

Definition: Kenpo uses both linear and circular movements with an emphasis on blending movements. Students are encouraged to alter movements to fit their personal style while maintaining guiding principles.

Origin: United States (Hawaii)

History: Kenpo was introduced to the Hawaiian islands by James Mitose in 1941 and Americanized by one of his students, William K.S. Chow. A student of Chow's, Ed Parker, then adapted the techniques to modern living and developed a highly organized system of American Kenpo.

☯ Kung-Fu (Wu Shu)

Definition: Kung-fu does not name one particular martial art but is a general classification for hundreds of Chinese martial arts styles. Schools are distinguished by what they emphasize and variations are broken down into such details as regions of origin, religious philosophies, family clans, military organizations, types of techniques, etc. **Wu Shu** is the official name for Chinese kung-fu. Many weapons are taught including sword, spear, and whip.

Origin: China

History: Kung-fu's exact founding date is disputed. Some records state 16th century B.C. while others state around 475 B.C. One legend describes how the emperor gave Bodhidharma the Shaolin Temple to use as a monastery. He developed kung-fu to increase the monks' abilities to handle long periods of prayer.

Major variations: Hsing-I, wing chun, white crane, drunken style, eagle claw system, hop gar, monkey style, praying mantis.

☯ Ninjutsu (Ninja)

Definition: Ninjutsu today is an art that practices stealth, deception and combat skills, including a wide variety of unusual weapons.

Origin: Japan

History: Ninjas were secret espionage experts skilled in weapons, explosives, medicine survival, combat and concealment techniques.

☯ Pentjak-Silat (Silat)

Definition: Pentjak-silat uses both armed and unarmed techniques in a system of flowing graceful movements.

Origin: Indonesia

History: Pentjak-Silat originated on the island of Sumatra. According to legend, it was developed by a woman who observed a deadly battle between a large bird and a tiger. She demonstrated their movements for her husband who began teaching them as the basis for this art.

☯ Taekwondo

Definition: Taekwondo is the art of hand and foot fighting which emphasizes training of the mind as well as the body. Though known for its spectacular kicks, the use of hand techniques is increasing. Taekwondo is one of the most common styles of martial arts taught in the United States today. It is the second martial art to be officially accepted as an Olympic sport.

Origin: Korea

History: It combines the ancient arts of subak and taekyon and includes the use of hyung (forms) to teach movements. In 1955, General Hong Hi Choi's suggested name for the art was accepted by noted martial arts masters and historians because it accurately described the use of hand and foot techniques in the art and it sounded like taekyon, Korea's ancient art. Jhoon Rhee is known as the father of American taekwondo, opening the first school in Texas in 1956.

☯ Tai-Chi

Definition: Tai-chi is a Chinese system of movement. The techniques are practiced slowly and include many circular, soft motions. Tai-chi ch'uan, from the north, focuses on chi as the source of power and force.

Origin: China

History: Tai chi is an art founded by Chen-Wong-Ting and learned solely by members of the Ch'en family.

Variations: Ch'eng, ch'en, and ch'uan. All tai chi styles are based on the original ch'en style.

☯ Tang Soo Do

Definition: This modern art form is based on the ancient Korean art of soo bahk do and the Chinese T'ang method. It combines hard and soft techniques and emphasizes the growth of maturity in the practitioner. Chuck Norris is a noted student of this art.

Origin: Korea

History: Grandmaster Hwang Kee founded tang soo do moo duk kwan, a classical martial art designed to develop the entire inner and outer person.

☯ Thai Boxing (Muay Thai)

Definition: It is Thailand's popular national sport and is a major tourist attraction. Records have been lost, but generally it is thought to have been founded prior to the 1500s.

Origin: Thailand

History: Although the practice of muay thai dates back centuries, the modern form of Thai boxing originated in the 1930's when fighters began wearing boxing gloves and following a uniform set of rules. Prior to the introduction of these limitations on what types of blows could be used, deaths in the ring were common.

Eclectic Arts

Many martial arts schools do not teach a single system. These eclectic schools combine what they consider the best elements of a variety of systems and form completely new styles. Some schools keep a traditional art as their base, adding to it as they see the necessity

The benefits of studying an eclectic style include the freedom to change when the instructor deems it necessary. Often more realistic than traditional styles, eclectic styles have adapted to today's world.

At the same time, the drawbacks to a true eclectic style are the lack of structure and the lack of one solid base. There is no real way to judge the quality of the instructor or the instructor's qualifications because there are no standards for comparison. Eclectic schools might not have or focus much of their teaching on philosophy and history.

Schools based on traditional styles have a common base from which to judge the quality of the instructor's knowledge and teaching style. Philosophy and history are important elements of a traditional school, and there is a common base of knowledge taught from one school to another. Some examples of eclectic styles you might encounter:

☯ **Aikikendo**
Momoji Sudoh combined techniques from aikido, jujutsu and karate for this art.

☯ **Kajukendo**
In 1947, five martial artists in Hawaii blended the arts of Chinese boxing, kenpo, judo, karate and jujutsu.

☯ **Lima Lama**
Aikido, kung-fu and boxing make up important elements of this art founded by Tino Tuilosega, an American martial artist of Polynesian heritage.

☯ **Kuk Sool Won**
Founded in 1966, Kuk Sool Won combines jujutsu, judo and karate. It is an effective system which can be used by women and the elderly.

Will My Child Learn to Use Weapons?

Whether your child will learn a weapon depends on the school you select. Some schools teach weapons and others don't. Some have established regular weapons classes which students can attend once they reach a certain rank. Schools also set a minimum age for weapons training based on the weapon taught and the method used to teach it.

Schools with no organized weapons training may offer occasional workshops or short courses. Other schools will teach a weapon not normally found within their martial art because they have someone in their school trained in that weapon.

The student learns weapons are an extension of the body. Training for certain traditional weapons can follow strict rituals and katas; while training for others is more free-flowing. Weapons training teaches control, spatial location, coordination, balance, timing and visualization.

Below are general descriptions of the most common weapons.

☯ Bo (Staff)

A long wooden staff used by warriors during feudal times. Originating in Okinawa, the six-foot bo is made of oak and is one-inch in diameter. The practitioner holds it in a two-handed grip to parry, thrust, and sweep. In martial arts tournaments, students can compete in weapons forms with the bo.

☯ Escrima

These are short (one to two feet) Philippine fighting sticks. The practitioner can fight with a single stick or with one in each hand. Used to block, parry and attack.

☯ Jo

Founded in Japan, a jo is a stick less than five-feet long and less than an inch wide. It is used to trip, throw and defend against attack. Practitioners practice katas (forms). The jo is often used in tournament weapons competitions.

☯ Kama

Originating from the sickle used in harvesting, the kama has a short wooden handle with a curved, seven-inch blade attached at a ninety degree angle a few inches from the tip. The martial artist learns how to use the weapon by practicing katas (forms) with wooden kamas. The practitioner uses a weapon in each hand since many of the reaping movements employ two kamas.

☯ Kung-Fu Broadsword

A large single-edged sword with a curved blade used in kung-fu forms. The practitioner can use one or two (one in each hand).

☯ Nunchaku

When weapons were outlawed, people improvised from the agricultural tools they had close at hand. Okinawans adapted the horse's bit into nunchaku. Nunchaku consists of two, approximately one-foot-long wooden pieces connected by chain or braided rope. The shape and length of wood in the handles varies.

☯ Sai

Probably founded in Indonesia (India, China, Malaysia also claim it), it is used most often in Okinawan fighting systems. It is a short, trident shaped, metal weapon. Two short, curved tines extend from the short center grip and point in the same direction as the long center rod.

☯ Sword

A sword can measure in length from 18 to 36 inches. Kung-fu (wu shu) uses many varieties of swords including hooked, single or double bladed. Differences occur in length, handles, and hand guards. Some of the sword varieties originating in Japan include the bokken, a wooden sword; the shinai, a multi-sectioned mock sword made of bamboo; and the katana which is over two feet in length and has an intricately decorated handle. The katana was used by Japanese samurai.

☯ Tonfa

The weapon was not originally a weapon but a handle for a millstone. The tonfa consists of a narrowing wooden shaft measuring up to twenty inches and used to guard the forearm. A short grip is placed at a right angle and about five inches from one end of the shaft. Practitioners most often use a tonfa in each hand. The tonfa is similar to the police baton, otherwise known as a PR-24.

4

Identifying Your Child's Needs

The school equipped with the most modern machines, locker rooms and showers might not be the best place for your child to learn the martial arts.

Selection of a martial arts school should be guided by the you and your child's priorities. For instance, if you're looking for self-defense skills, the best teacher in the state might be teaching twice a week in a local high school, not at the spacious school just built down the street.

The right martial arts school for your child is the one that provides a positive place for them to grow.

What Are My Child's Priorities?

To establish priorities, you must weigh both your child's interests and your goals for your son or daughter.

Learning discipline and good self-defense skills, or enjoying a recreational, challenging activity are some of the reasons parents want their children to study the martial arts.

Your child might want to meet new friends. Martial arts classes can connect people from a variety of backgrounds with a common ground from which to build friendships. If your child has a strong desire to compete, the martial arts offer many tournaments.

Or if your child wants to pursue an individual athletic activity, the martial arts provide an arena in which children can challenge themselves, improve, and showcase their skills.

What Are My Priorities?

If your child enjoys the martial arts experience, it is an indication that you have considered your own needs in addition to their's. If parents are happy, children are happy.

An important first step is finances. Prices for classes vary widely and might include extras such as registration, association membership fees, school fees, etc.

You will drive your child to the school two to three times a week in all kinds of weather. Travel time must be taken into consideration, especially during winter weather conditions.

The location of the school is also important. Is it convenient, safe, easy to reach? In addition, classes should be offered at times convenient for both you and your child.

Can Children With Disabilities Learn a Martial Art?

"Every child has more abilities than disabilities" is a favorite saying of Charles Peterson, Director of the Center for Adaptive Education and Assistive Technology at St. Norbert College, and a foster parent of over 140 children, most of them with multiple disabilities.

Parents of children with disabilities often wonder whether their children can participate in the martial arts. How far children advance will depend on them and their particular abilities as well as the commitments of their instructors and parents.

In cases of obvious limitations, talk with instructors at different schools to find one who is willing to use the child's abilities to work around limitations, who is willing to look beyond the disability and see the inner child. Children may be different on the outside, but on the inside they are all little girls or little boys. They hurt, cry, dream and laugh like everyone else.

Your child may need extra support in order to learn and progress, possibly weekly private lessons. Instructors interested in the unique challenges of teaching children with special needs will research and try creative teaching methods adapted to your child's particular limitations. They will be willing to work with your child's strengths to improve the deficits.

You may need to consider whether your child will benefit from pre-teaching. If you can enroll in classes before your child, you can supplement class instruction with practice sessions at home. Or you might consider making arrangements with an upper belt to review techniques with your child before classes.

You must be willing to support instructors when they encourage your child to try something new thta they feel is legitimately within your child's range of ability.

Children who are blind or nearly blind need someone to use the hand-over-hand method with them in addition to explaining how to form a fist and punch. Hearing impaired students benefit from watching the instructor demonstrate the techniques or the next activity.

"The material is the same," said a martial arts instructor who began teaching people with disabilities over 28 years ago. "The methodology for teaching the material is different. It's more tactile, requires more touching, more positioning of the bodies, and guiding of arms, hands, and legs."

Parents' insights into how their children function can prove invaluable to instructors. You can observe classes, take notes, and offer suggestions. "Parents know what vocabulary the child responds to, what phrasing to use," said an instructor who works closely with parents. "They know what motivates the children and what doesn't motivate them."

Children who have trouble remembering or following directions, benefit from the martial arts' rigid class structure. Standing next to other students gives them someone to follow. The constant repetition of format: warm-ups, stretching, techniques, and cool-down, provides a structure they soon will recognize and expect.

You know if your child can respond appropriately to questions or if, for example, he or she must demonstrate a stance to show it has been learned.

Repetition is beneficial to those students who may have poor short term memory. Like riding a bicycle, once these skills are learned, they usually are not forgotten.

Many children don't like change. While much of the class is structured, a variety of activities are used to teach different skills. You can prepare your child to be ready for what the class lesson will cover in addition to the instructor's reminder at the beginning of class. When a promotion is scheduled, you and the instructor can describe the difference between classes and promotions.

Martial arts is taught using the building block method, and many children respond well to the breakdown of techniques into concrete and functional steps.

The instructor usually gives concise commands and directions. When longer explanations are used, children can follow the person standing next to them. Some children respond well when the instructor demonstrates a series of movements while facing the same direction as the children.

Creative methods such as putting a small mark on one of the hands can be suggested to the instructor if your child has difficulty understanding the concepts of left and right. This way, your child will always know which direction to turn or which hand to use for an exercise.

Some children are extremely strong physically, but do not realize it and are unable to control their strength. Knowing this in advance helps the instructor be aware of what to watch for.

Self-defense is a concept some children will never master. They will never develop defensive reactions such as putting up an arm to block. One instructor, recognizing this in a student, only allowed the child to spar once in awhile and then only with the instructor as his partner.

Some children have balance problems which cannot be fixed or improved with practice. For others, martial arts activities will help improve their balance. Since ear infections can affect a child's usual balancing abilities and performance in class, tell your instructor if your child has an ear infection.

An instructor who works with vision impaired children and others with balance problems said he places his finger at a point in the child's lower back when the child practices a kick. This helps the body create a "motor memory" for a balanced technique.

He explained children with disabilities should take a minimum of three trial lessons and parents should observe the classes. "The school should have its best teachers teaching. These children are not a training ground for new instructors."

The benefits can be enormous. One child with autism could perform a task with three commands when he started. After a while he could do a task with four commands and worked his way up to performing a task with six commands.

Martial arts creates an inclusive environment in which many children with disabilities can participate and work out in class next to children without disabilities.

Can Children With Disabilities Participate in Tournaments?

Some tournaments offer Physically Challenged divisions in which people with disabilities can compete against each other. These divisions are optional, not mandatory, and aren't offered in all events—generally in forms and sometimes in sparring.

"The children benefit in the same ways all children can benefit from tournaments," said an instructor with 25 to 30 children with disabilities in his school, many of whom compete. "They travel, meet new friends, perform to the best of their abilities, and win trophies."

In many cases, the instructor is allowed to be in the ring with the child during the routine. The instructor does the routine with the student, providing a mirror the student can shadow. In other cases, the instructor can stand on the side of the ring to support the child.

Some tournaments award trophies or medals to all students participating in the physically challenged division. Other tournaments award trophies to only the winning students.

"My personal feeling," the instructor said, "is to give them all something. One first place, one second place, one third place, and five people tied for fourth place. It gives them something tangible to walk out with and rewards them for performing to the maximum of their ability. It doesn't diminish the value of the trophy or the value of place."

Some tournaments are rated and competitors can earn points toward state or national championships in the Physically Challenged divisions.

Does Martial Arts Benefit Children with ADHD?

Increasingly, children are being diagnosed with Attention Deficit Hyperactive Disorders which are neurobiological disorders. For many affected youngsters, the martial arts has proven to be extremely successful in providing a structured framework which helps them learn to function and feel good about themselves.

A martial arts instructor who studied attention deficit hyperactive disorders to help prepare other instructors at the school, explained, "Attention Deficit is like having 47 things coming into your mind at all times. They cannot complete the entire thought process before another comes in."

Education professionals often quote Richard D. Lavoie, M.A., M.Ed., Executive Director of the Riverview School, East Sandwich, Massachusetts, from the award winning video, *How Difficult Can This Be? Understanding Learning Disabilities, The F.A.T. City Workshop.* He described Attention Deficit Hyperactive Disorders as like having a television set in the brain with the channels changing all the time and someone else controlling the remote control.

Since all sounds and movements have the same impact and nothing is filtered out, these children have a hard time staying focused. These are neurobiological disorders; the children are not purposely trying to disobey or act out. Attention Deficit children react to the moment. Medication is sometimes necessary and helps many enormously. People diagnosed with attention deficit never outgrow these chemical imbalances. As they progress into adulthood, they learn to adjust and compensate for the symptoms.

The martial arts provides a structured, fast-paced format which helps these children stay on track. The straight lines in which they stand according to rank and the formal manner with which they address upper belts and instructors all help them stay focused. Children learn what to expect and find comfort and room to grow within the structure. They are constantly moving and are continually mentally challenged.

"The martial arts stretched his level of concentration," said a mother of a child diagnosed with Attention Deficit Hyperactive Disorder. "He responded very well to encouragement from the instructor."

Good teaching methods apply to all children whether or not they have disorders. Instructors must stand where all students can see and focus on them. They must be consistent in their expectations and in their willingness to help all children reach their full potential.

Many children with disabilities have taken the martial arts and succeeded, even becoming state and national champions. While it takes more effort on the part of parents, instructors and children, the benefits of martial arts philosophies and structures which can be used in the children's everyday lives are well worth it.

Part 2

Finding the Right School

5

Choosing a School

The choice of a martial arts school can play an important part in the physical and emotional development of your child and impact whether they have an enjoyable experience. Children thrive in positive learning environments. A pleasant, supportive atmosphere increases their desire to return to lessons again and again and to keep practicing. A school that is a "good fit" with your child will contribute to his or her success in the martial arts.

A successful experience starts with clarifying what you and your child hope to attain from studying the martial arts. Goals can include gaining self-defense skills, confidence, friends, trophies, or a black belt, to just having fun. As a parent, your personal commitments will include finances and time.

Because your child will be influenced by the school's behavior and attitude, the school's standards of behavior and its overall attitude are important aspects to consider for a good fit. By observing its students in and out of class, you can determine the school's attitude and atmosphere.

What Is Expected From Students?

"I ask if their child knows their right from their left," said a master instructor with twenty-three years teaching experience. "If so, I can teach them taekwondo."

Most schools establish a minimum starting age. Some will not enroll anyone under the age of five, while others will allow four-year olds or younger to begin lessons.

Instructors usually want to meet with parents and children before enrolling youngsters. If a child is five or younger, some instructors will test the child's readiness to learn by taking them through a few movements.

You can try a few simple activities at home to test your child's readiness to study the martial arts. To measure the level of self-control, ask your child to pretend to be a statue and to look straight ahead at an object. When your child is in place, walk to another part of the room and quietly observe for a few minutes to see if your child stands in the statue pose or moves and looks around.

Children should understand the basic concepts of motion and direction such as left/right and forward/backward. To measure your child's understanding, ask him or her to step to the right and then to the left, to step forward and pick up the left foot, and to step backward and pick up the right foot. If "step forward" or "step back" are too complicated, it is better to wait. Waiting will increase your child's chances of enjoying a successful experience.

Beginning children's classes can range from 30 to 40 minutes long. Generally, children starting at age seven or later can handle longer classes of 50 to 60 minutes.

Children should be in their teens before beginning training for full-contact competitive events. Contact training requires emotional maturity, commitment, proper breathing, balance, focus, concentration, and correct technique. In contact sparring, competitors cannot become angry when they are hit. They have to fight strategically, controlling their emotions and looking for openings.

Non-contact and light-contact training can begin earlier. This will help children develop control, speed, and technique.

Forms (prearranged routines) competition can begin at any age. Young children often compete with forms they learn in class. As they become more skilled, the instructor may create a specialized competition form for them. Sometimes, students create their own competition forms.

How Will My Child Learn All Those Complicated Looking Moves?

Most children learn by mastering one step at a time and developing a base of knowledge. Martial arts basics can include some stances, blocks, punches, joint locks, kicks, proper breathing, balance, and concentration.

After learning the fundamentals, children are expected to practice and fine tune the basic techniques and develop combinations. The techniques should become second nature. They learn about the culture and history of their martial art's country of origin and study the art's philosophy. They add one small bit of knowledge at a time until it all connects and makes sense. This can take time and requires patience from parents and children.

At first, students of all ages tend to feel lost. They look at others in the class and wonder if they'll ever learn. But they do. Because techniques are broken down into movements and practiced again and again, everyone can learn.

Once children recognize they are improving, their self-confidence builds, and they are more eager to try new and more difficult techniques.

Can My Child Learn More Than One Martial Art at a Time?

After achieving black belt, children can study and learn strengths of other styles. Soon, they'll add their favorite techniques from other styles to their skill base.

Many schools that teach one basic martial art also include techniques from other arts. "Each art has good and bad points," said an instructor. "It's important not to take a hard line, but to have a blend and expose students to other techniques, and to be able to retreat to ground zero—something solid, like the main martial art."

Some instructors with a background of more than one martial art incorporate curriculum into their black belt classes which enable students to learn another martial art while they are doing further training in their primary martial art.

How Can I Compare the Different Styles?

Martial arts styles vary. Some are graceful and fluid, others are linear and angular. If your community offers options such as karate, taekwondo, aikido and tai chi, visit the schools and observe the different styles. Public demonstrations provide enjoyable opportunities to evaluate styles. Open tournaments bring together martial artists of many styles into one arena, and you and your child can compare the styles at one time. Since a lot of time is spent learning a martial art, select an art with movements that appeal to you.

Once you select a certain martial art, visit several schools in your area that teach that style. Even though the schools teach similar techniques, they will differ on what aspect of the martial arts they emphasize as well as on their overall philosophy and teaching style.

While one taekwondo school will focus on forms and self-defense with some free-sparring, another may concentrate primarily on competitive free-sparring. Look for a balance of fitness, forms, self-defense, free-sparring, culture, fun activities and discipline. Teaching skills without discipline or understanding of tradition often produces talented bullies, not martial artists.

Schools vary in location as well as in their emphasis. Facilities are located downtown, in shopping malls, in industrial parks and in residential areas. Classes can be taught anywhere. Many classes are taught in YWCAs and YMCAs or in school gymnasïums. Many great instructors, including Bruce Lee, taught lessons on their driveways until they could rent facilities.

How well students know and perform the material is a sign of the quality of the instruction. You can develop a sense of the school's attitude toward the art and teaching by how well students workout in class.

Are Girls Welcome?

Even today, many girls view physical activity, especially a sport that involves contact, as unfeminine. If they are in the confusing middle school years, it can be harder for them to participate in a martial art.

Girls are rarely taught to fight. Granted, many growing up with older brothers have learned how to throw a punch and to stand up for themselves. But, this is not self-defense.

Martial arts is about mastering control of one's mind and body, of learning the basics of blocking and punching, of learning to react with controlled self-defense, not uncontrolled emotion.

Both males and females are taught how to punch, and once it's mastered, a girl won't hear, "You punch like a girl." The actual act of learning how to block and use one's hands and feet for self-defense, creates a positive mental attitude that can lead a child to think "I'm worth fighting for." A confident attitude leads to assertive behavior and can decrease the "victim" persona.

Young girls often look up to female black belts as role models and may find it easier to approach them. Many of these black belts have learned that a lot of the self-defense techniques are taught from a man's viewpoint and aren't necessarily effective techniques for either women or children. Using their experience, they can teach how they have adjusted the techniques so they work for younger, shorter, and weaker persons.

How Can I Find Classes In My Area?

When looking for a martial arts school, word of mouth remains one of the most effective methods of identifying quality schools. With the boom of children entering the martial arts, it's possible your child has friends studying somewhere. Talk to the friends' parents and discover where their children go and if they recommend the school. Coworkers who take martial arts classes may be able to suggest schools that are suitable for children.

Almost every city has special celebrations which can be showcases for local talents and businesses including martial arts schools. In addition, schools often give demonstrations in a public place such as a school or shopping mall.

The demonstrations involve young and old students, all working together to perform ancient techniques to the best of their abilities. Demos can include forms, entertaining skits, self-defense, step-sparring, weapons; whatever the school decides to highlight. After the performance, students might pass out special introductory offer coupons and answer questions.

Local YMCAs and YWCAs, colleges and universities, and boys and girls clubs normally offer classes. A six-week class can provide strong clues as to whether your child is really interested in the martial arts or if the arts are just a passing fancy.

City parks and recreation departments often offer martial arts classes and self-defense workshops as special summer or year-round programs.

Martial arts clubs, lacking their own facilities, often find space to rent in large buildings such as school gymnasiums or dance schools, or they might affiliate with health clubs.

Martial arts schools advertise introductory specials in daily or weekly newspapers, use inserts (stuffers), or even print self-stick notes which are attached to the front page of the paper. Specials can be advertised over the radio, on billboards, and on the school's recorded phone message.

Some free or low cost trial offers include a uniform. All special introductory offers give you and your child the chance to step into the school and evaluate the actual classes.

The yellow pages of telephone books list commercial schools under the headings "Martial Arts Instruction" or "Karate Instruction." In addition to the school's name, address and phone number, a display ad on the same page may tell you what the school's focus is, the instructor's background, and the age groups are taught.

Eventually, any serious study of the martial arts will require obtaining a skilled, committed martial artist as an instructor. He or she will most likely be found in a commercial school.

Sources of Information About Schools in Your Area:

✓ Parents of your child's friends

✓ Co-workers

✓ Demonstrations at fairs, festivals or shopping malls

✓ Local clubs like YMCA/YWCA, health clubs, girls/boys clubs

✓ Parks and Recreation departments

✓ Yellow Pages

✓ Newspaper advertisements

How Should I Approach a School for Information?

Once schools are identified, call the owners, or head instructors. Find out what the schools emphasize in their classes and what they hope children will learn by taking lessons in their facility. Most schools encourage a visit. These calls can give you a feel for the schools and their styles.

Follow-up telephone inquiries with calls to the local Better Business Bureau and Bureau of Consumer Affairs. Eliminate schools with a number of unresolved complaints. Schools which obviously do not fulfill the goals identified by you and your child can also be eliminated. For schools that you cannot gather details about, a visit to the facility will give more information. The quality of the facility and its equipment, the price of lessons, and the atmosphere vary from school to school. You may not be able to judge these factors accurately over the phone.

What's Next?

The next step entails touring the facilities. During the tour, identify the features you like the most and try to find a school which combines most of these features. Among the features to consider are:

☐ Location

Schools can be found anywhere: a newly constructed facility, a storefront, a shopping mall, a school building, or a warehouse.

If the facility is in a business district, note which businesses are open when your child takes lessons. If there are restaurants and bars nearby, return at the time of classes and observe the clientele. If you are unsure about the safety of any location, even a residential neighborhood, obtain a crime report for that area from the police.

☐ Parking/Lighting

Many schools will have an adjoining parking lot, access to one within a block or simply offer street parking. You will have to decide whether the parking is adequate and appears safe.

Parking lots and streets should be well-lit. Since many of the lessons are taught after school or in the evening, it will probably be dark at the end of lessons—especially in the winter.

Schools are required to have more than one exit in case of emergency. The exit might not be used often, but it must be unlocked so students can leave through it if necessary. Note what is outside all exits: a street, parking lot, or other stores and businesses.

☐ Travel Time

Travel time must be taken into consideration and be within a family's normal driving range. For example, some families are used to driving 30 minutes to activities, others are used to driving 15 minutes. The closer a school is to your home, the more convenient it is and the less time it adds to your weekly chauffeuring.

❏ Cleanliness

A clean and well-maintained facility will add to the experience. It's a positive sign if students and staff treat the school facility with respect and help keep it clean. It's also a sign of the instructor's attention to detail.

❏ Dressing Rooms

The dressing rooms, showers, lockers, and bathrooms should be clean. While dressing rooms are necessary, it is not necessary for schools to offer showers and lockers. If they provide individual lockers, they may not be available for each class but may be rented for a length of time. Each family will have to decide how important showers and lockers are to fulfilling their goals.

Dressing rooms easily accessible from the waiting room, where you can see who goes in and out, are more secure than rooms located in a different area of the building.

❏ Workout Areas

Workout areas should be large enough for students to practice without running into each other. Support columns in the rooms should be surrounded by padding.

The floors in the workout rooms can vary from wood to tile, mats to carpeting. All should be clean and in good condition.

Because of their energy, enthusiasm, and growing muscles, children can be more prone to injuries than adults who usually take the time to stretch before class. Some instructors prefer carpeting, especially padded carpeting, or mats to help protect students' growing bodies, while others prefer tile or wood floors.

❏ Waiting Room

Unless you are taking lessons with your child, you will spend a lot of time in the waiting room. This is a more pleasant experience if the room is large, clean, adequately ventilated and inviting with enough chairs so you can sit comfortably. Some instructors provide a box of toys, coloring books and crayons for younger brothers and sisters to play with. Waiting rooms which are separated from the workout room should have a large window or an open doorway through which you can observe the class. In cases such as schools with classes in a gymnasium, you might find yourself sitting right on the sidelines.

❐ Concessions

Many schools supply vending machines filled with soft drinks and candy. Children benefit more if schools have installed water fountains.

❐ Equipment

Martial arts workout equipment can include punching bags, stretching equipment, cycles, treadmills, weight machines, mats, and targets. All equipment should be clean and in good condition, not ripped or broken.

Some of these, especially the targets, mats and punching bags will be found within the workout room. Exercise equipment can be located in a separate area from the workout room. Signs posted by the machines should outline rules for correct usage and how old children must be before they can use the machines. Children should be supervised when they use equipment.

School Tour Checklist:

✓ Location: Safe neighborhood? Neighboring businesses?

✓ Parking: Close by? Safe to walk to at night?

✓ Outdoor Lighting: Parking lot and surroundings well lit?

✓ Travel Time: Close enough to home?

✓ Cleanliness: School clean inside?

✓ Dressing Rooms: Safe location? Well maintained?

✓ Workout areas: Safe floors? Poles padded?

✓ Waiting Room: Comfortable? View to workout area?

✓ Concessions: Water fountain available?

✓ Equipment: In good repair? Instructions posted?

How Can You Spot a Good Instructor?

By watching and listening to how the instructor directs and works with children in a class, you can decide whether the instructor is telling students what needs to be done in a supportive, understandable manner. The best instructors are willing to explain and answer questions and will not criticize or make fun of the children for asking.

Observing interactions between the instructor and students before and after class can provide you with more clues as to whether the instructor likes children. Does the instructor make an effort to talk with the students as well as their younger brothers and sisters or does he or she disappear into an office?

A valuable instructor is one who is willing to honestly and patiently discuss children's progress with parents and does not just brush aside parents' concerns and questions. An instructor who knows who your child is, cares about your child's progress, and is committed to helping your child improve will contribute greatly to your child's overall experience in the martial arts.

The instructor as well as other adult students in the school will become role models for the children. The conduct, neatness, and cleanliness of the instructors reflects how much they respect themselves, the school and the students. Instructors don't have to be in perfect shape, especially those who are older, but they should make an effort to stay physically fit and be able to correctly demonstrate techniques.

Instructors should be black belts. Their qualifications include where and how long they have taught as well as the number of years they have studied and where. They might have other teaching experiences either directly related to the martial arts (such as self-defense workshops) or indirectly such as in the educational system.

A real advantage for any parent and child is a martial arts instructor who respects knowledge and encourages students to pursue it. In addition to skills, the instructor teaches terminology, suggests resource materials, asks and answers questions about the art's philosophy and basic history. As one instructor stated, "It's really important that the art is more than kicks and punches."

Are High Pressure Sales Tactics Common?

The instructor needs to successfully run a business in order to have a place to teach, and he or she needs a strong desire and commitment to teaching students in order to have a business. An instructor who is a martial artist as well as an honorable entrepreneur will combine these two needs into a well-run school in which students are more likely to experience success.

However, you might run into an instructor who concentrates on signing up new students rather than teaching the ones already enrolled. To them, the business aspect is most important, and they will use whatever tactics work to get your signature.

A father, describing his first meeting with an instructor, explained how the instructor left the class for a half-hour to greet him and his child and to sell him a membership contract.

"It's high pressure," the father said. "You feel the class is waiting to start up again, and you're holding it up!"

An instruction oriented school implements business procedures which allow the instructor to spend his or her time teaching. The school has a telephone answering machine and someone covering the office. The instructor is not expected to leave classes while they are in session. Someone else, possibly an office manager or an outside firm, sends out the bills.

When the instructor's focus is primarily on education, not finances, your child will remain important to the instructor longer than the first meeting and lesson. Your child benefits when the instructor concentrates on providing a good education through an efficiently run business.

How Can You Tell If a School Has a Long-Term Success Record?

The rank of black belt is a beginning, not an end or a graduation. Students need to understand this. If the school offers opportunities for advanced study of the martial arts, students are more likely to grasp that concept.

Watching his 12-year old son study for his upcoming black belt test, a father asked him what he had to know.

"Everything," the son replied.

"Then what are you going to study when you're a black belt?"

"Everything else," the young student said.

Schools providing advanced study for black belts will have a number of black belts in classes. Your child has more potential for growth in the martial arts if there are a number of black belts studying in the school. Each person has different strengths to share, and your child benefits from this diversity.

Long established schools with a lot of new students and only a few black belts or advanced students have retention problems. A school maintaining the positive interest, enthusiasm and education of its upper belts is a serious, well-grounded concern.

Narrowing Down the Choices

1. Does the instructor accurately evaluate your child's readiness?

2. Does the school treat boys and girls equally?

3. Does the school meet your criteria on the school tour checklist? (page 78)

4. Is the instructor well qualified?

5. Does the school emphasize teaching over making money?

6. Does the school appear to have a long-term success record?

If you can answer yes to the above questions, this is a school worth taking a closer look at.

6

Asking the Right Questions

During the initial visit, you should have the opportunity to ask the instructor a number of questions about his or her background, credentials and philosophy of teaching, as well as the instructor's goals for the school.

What Are the Instructor's Credentials?

Knowing more about the instructor's background, the events which steered the instructor toward the martial arts and the reasons he or she stayed in the arts, can provide some information about his or her basic philosophy toward the martial arts, teaching, and life.

Find out how many years and at what locations the instructor has studied and taught. Has the instructor supplemented his or her study of the martial arts with workshops, seminars and conferences?

Children enjoy learning from instructors who like the challenges of teaching their age and rank level; who research various teaching methods; and who know a lot about the learning styles and abilities of children.

Just as certificates grace a doctor's office walls and highlight the doctor's academic qualifications, the martial art facility's office walls can contain black belt certificates, medals, pictures, and honors the instructor and the school have received. Certificates and thank you letters recognize the school's community outreach activities. Achievement certificates highlight special, intensive training seminars and workshops the instructor has attended.

The dates on the black belt certificates can provide information such as how many years of experience the instructor has had at various black belt levels. Credentials can be questioned if, for example, an instructor has a third degree black belt and the second degree certificate was attained less than a year before. As a general rule, it takes approximately two years to progress from first to second degree, three years from second to third degree, four years from third to fourth degree and so on. While it can take longer to progress from rank to rank, a shorter promotion period may indicate rank that was "bought" rather than earned.

If the recognition certificates and thank you letters were written years ago, it could be a sign the instructors are no longer really interested in teaching the martial arts. This may be something they have not yet realized themselves. An enthusiastic, dedicated instructor will lead active classes, get students involved in the community, and help keep children interested.

While it isn't necessary to have a college degree in order to teach good classes, whether the instructor has one or not can shed some light on his or her background and philosophy toward education in general.

An instructor who specializes in one or two of the martial arts and believes in imparting history and philosophy to the students can add immensely to the development of your child as a martial artist and a person. Be wary of those who view the arts simply as a sport. As one instructor observed, "To keep the martial art what the martial art really is, it needs roots. If we lose too much history, it just becomes a kick boxing school."

Some instructors are ranked or have been ranked on the regional or national competition circuit. If your child is interested in competing, he or she will benefit directly from an instructor who knows the competition circuit and can train students to compete successfully. Many schools proudly display trophies won by instructors as well as students. Competition is a generally accepted manner in which to demonstrate and test one's skill. Not all skilled martial artists compete or feel the need to do so. It's not necessary to have competition experience in order to be a good instructor. What is necessary is the desire and ability to teach and impart skills and knowledge to others.

Federations and chains of schools abound in the martial arts. Some schools belong to federations or are part of a chain, while others are not. Sometimes, an instructor will expand locally, creating his or her own "chain." Ultimately, it is a school's good, solid reputation which will figure most in whether your child enjoys a successful experience in the martial arts rather than whether the school belongs to a federation or chain.

What Is the Instructor's Teaching Philosophy?

A taekwondo instructor once observed that if the instructor is to make a good impression upon a student, it's up to the instructor to teach at the student's level.

People have different learning styles. Some learn best by listening while others are visual learners and have to see something in print or write it down before they remember it. Others have to repeat something many times before they learn it. A good instructor is prepared to teach so that all students can learn, no matter what their style.

A mother and son preparing for their black belt tests discovered their differences. When they worked with a black belt after class, the mother found she had to repeat a technique many times. The son listened, performed it once or twice and remembered it.

The most effective method to teach techniques is to combine an explanation with a demonstration of the movements. By breaking complicated procedures into manageable steps, children and adults can learn new skills. This is demonstrated by the success of the Suzuki method of teaching music and the number of three- and four-year old violinists in its programs. The Montessori school of education demonstrates exactly how a project is to be completed and achieves successful results.

Demonstrating a technique, explaining its purpose, and asking students to imitate the instructor's movements clarifies the technique in children's minds. While we might all dream of learning by osmosis, practice (and lots of it) is necessary for success.

The instructor must have control over the class. The most successful classes have relaxed and accepting atmospheres in which students are encouraged to master techniques with positive input from the instructor. Children and adults learn best when they feel secure in class, knowing the instructor won't allow anyone to verbally or physically hurt them. Too much fear or negative pressure to succeed can lead to tenseness and panic. Once this happens, minds block learning and nothing can enter.

A woman, observing an alternative, academic classroom, noticed some children walking around and talking, while others worked by themselves or in small groups. As a former teacher, she recognized that while the class looked loose and chaotic, it was extremely organized and controlled. Most children in this type of controlled, relaxed atmosphere read a year before their counterparts in traditional schools.

Children thrive when they are rewarded for their effort, not just their successes. They want people whose opinion they respect to acknowledge these efforts. Not everyone has the same abilities and capabilities. Not everyone can be an athletic star. Those who are complimented on their efforts find a reason to keep trying to improve and work to the best of their abilities. Compliments on their effort and their techniques should be combined with critiques on what they can change to improve. The feedback must be encouraging, specific and honest.

The master or head instructor generally doesn't teach all classes. After talking with the instructor, ask to talk with the person who teaches children's classes. Discover what your child's potential instructor envisions as his or her goals for the classes. Do these goals correspond to the school's overall philosophy?

What Ranking System Is Used?

Traditionally, ranking systems didn't exist. Today, belts are symbols of rank, a measure of what has been learned as well as a motivational tool, giving children something tangible to work for. Observers can gain an idea of how much training students have had by the color of their belts.

Each student begins as a white belt. Most schools establish requirements which must be met before students test for the next rank or belt level. For instance, a certain number of classes must be attended and certain skills must be learned before testing. A system of ten belt levels leading up to black belt is common. A great deal more or less ranks to black belt should be suspect.

(*Note*: Aikido clubs following the standards set by the U.S. Aikido Federation have only five beginner ranks before reaching black belt. But these ranks, 5th kyu to 1st kyu, are for adults. Children will start at 10th kyu and work their way up to 6th kyu. Each kyu has three levels, e.g. 10-C, 10-B, 10-A, 9-C, 9-B, and so on. At schools which test twice a year, it would take eight years to get through five kyus. Often by that time, the child who started at six- or seven-years old is now a teenager of 14 or 15 and ready to test for the 5th kyu. An aikido instructor with 17 years of study explained that in some schools children can receive a double promotion, skipping some levels, so that it doesn't take the full eight years. In schools which hold more than two promotions a year and award double promotions, a child of six or seven might reach 6th kyu at too young of an age. In those cases, the instructor will hold the child at the top children's level for a year or two, before giving special permission to test for adult rank. "By that time, they'd probably be much better than most adult beginners testing for that rank, anyway," he said.)

Some schools list the skills and knowledge required for each rank. Others are more informal and tell students this information during classes. Some schools pass out a pamphlet and don't refer to it again until students test for black belt. Clarify which method the instructor uses. Ideally, students receive written as well as verbal information.

Schools establish their own class schedules and determine how many classes per week are open to beginners. These openings may easily fit into your family's schedule or require some modification on your part.

What Are the Instructor's Goals?

The instructor establishes the underlying philosophy and goals of the school's program, usually based on the martial art's and instructor's philosophies. Most people won't directly admit they don't teach sportsmanship or values such as proper use of the martial arts. Some simply point out that as role models they lead the way and students are expected to emulate them, and beyond that, the instructors feel they don't have to verbalize any beliefs or philosophy. They may not be able to express the underlying philosophy of their martial art for many reasons: they aren't verbal, they aren't interested, they never learned it, etc. Others can talk at length about their beliefs, but is what they say in line with how they act and how they conduct classes? Based on your observations, you can decide whether the instructor is a good role model for your child.

A written mission statement can show that much thought has gone into setting the school's goals. The statement should be available to any student. It is a tool you can use to evaluate whether the instructor is fulfilling what he or she established in the beginning. As the years pass, the instructor can refer to the statement and see if the activities, teaching structure, and his or her attitude toward teaching is still in line with the school's original mission or if adjustments need to be made.

Some programs emphasize participation, fun and personal growth while others emphasize winning. Schools can focus on teaching forms, self-defense, competition strategies, or fighting skills. Some are sport schools and don't emphasize philosophy, history and terminology, only techniques.

After determining goals for the school, the instructor establishes and implements educational procedures which will enable the goals to be reached. The philosophy and procedures vary from school to school.

Programs emphasizing personal improvement and personal satisfaction often institute class report cards which track children's attitudes and efforts in class. Children learn there is more than one way to be successful and that a positive attitude contributes to success.

Others believe students with the most trophies are the most successful. They see the child's success as a reflection of the quality of their school and of themselves, so winning is most important.

Some instructors allow children to test for their next belt when they aren't ready. Instructors couch this in the belief that children will stop trying if they aren't allowed to test.

But children sense when the instructor is not sincere and often attribute the instructor's decision to a lack of faith in their abilities. Children perceive this as due to their own failings and inabilities, not as a fault of the instructor. On the other hand, if an instructor expects children to do well and establishes an atmosphere which promotes this, children will succeed. Studies of at-risk children demonstrate time and time again that children rise to high expectations.

The instructor's attitudes and philosophies toward the art and other people will often be adopted by students. Parents of current students can describe to you their impressions of the instructor's values and beliefs and what the instructor has taught their children. By selecting an instructor whose values are similar to yours, you will find additional support for the values you have taught your child.

What Does the Curriculum Consist Of?

Once a style has been selected, parents can look at the curriculum and the way it's taught. Consistent curriculum ensures students at each rank are taught the same information. A written list of skills and knowledge required at each belt level helps students learn and prepare for promotions.

☆ Beginning Classes

White belt classes can include students of all ages, from young children to grandparents. Some schools hold beginner classes which are open to children only; beginning adults and teens attend at other times. Often classes are divided into belt levels. In which case, you may see an 11 year old or an adult white belt in the same class as a five-year old white belt.

☆ Adjusting Curriculum

The learning curve for a five-year old is usually steeper than the curve for an eleven-year old. Most eleven-year olds will probably be able to perform good techniques sooner than a five-year old, because eleven-year olds are more developed physically and have a greater understanding of what they're doing.

Since everyone does not learn in the same manner or at the same rate, it is most effective to teach the curriculum in as many ways as possible in order to help everyone learn. It's also good to modify the curriculum so it is appropriate for children ages four to six-years, seven to nine-years, and ten to twelve-years who are attending the same class. The self-defense curriculum taught to twelve-year olds differs from what should be taught to children four to six-years old.

☆ Multi-Age Classrooms and the Martial Arts

Many school systems across the United States are looking into and implementing multi-age classrooms. A multi-age classroom has more than one teacher to enable them to address the needs of all children. The teachers use a variety of teaching methods, allowing children to learn at their own speed. This is beneficial to many who might excel in some areas and need more time to learn skills in other areas. The partnering teachers create the curriculum and serve as the unifying force in the classroom. They encourage students to share their knowledge and help one another. This reinforces the teaching student's knowledge and helps the learning student.

The martial arts classroom can be an excellent example of a multi-age academic classroom. The instructor creates the lesson plans, using different methods to teach one skill. He or she arranges the class structure so students have opportunities to teach and learn from one another. One or more assistant instructors help teach beginner classes so all children have help learning the skills.

☆ Importance of Repetitive Curriculum

The basic martial arts curriculum must repeat itself even as it moves forward and covers new ground. Each class should allow time for students to practice skills they have learned as well as time for them to learn progressively more difficult curriculum. This allows everyone to advance, including black belts. Students who reach black belt do not want to stagnate. This process enables them to continue growing in the martial arts.

A child who achieves black belt at age eleven has room for improvement and much more to learn. How well children perform the skills relates to how much maturing their bodies have done. Girls will reach their adult potential during early adolescence, and boys will generally reach their adult skill potential in later adolescence.

What Are the School's Safety Rules for Free-Sparring?

Martial arts teaches fighting skills with the ultimate goal of not ever having to fight.

Free-sparring is practice fighting. In the best scenarios, children and their partners will use this time in a give-and-take manner. This trust enables them to practice blocking techniques and counterattacks. It teaches them to develop into thinking fighters, to learn what to look for, what to expect from certain attacks and blocks, and how to react. It helps children learn that for some techniques and situations the best action is to get out of the way.

Some schools (and they may not even realize it) are fighting schools. Students are taught to attack, to overpower their opponent. Students are not taught to block, to test and evaluate what their opponent/partner is doing and to adjust their fighting style accordingly.

Many schools set their own free-sparring safety rules, usually based on rules accepted by their style or established for competition. These include rules pertaining to rank and age which apply to all students who spar with a lower ranking or younger student.

For instance, children ages six to eight, can be limited to non-contact fighting. This enables them to learn techniques and practice speed and reaction time without fear of getting hurt by another student.

Controlled or light contact is often implemented for those ages eight to twelve, and full contact can be practiced in the teens. Some schools will not teach free-sparring to the lowest belts, but wait until they learn basic skills and are used to class routine.

Before sparring, instructors will inform students how much contact will be allowed and remind them of the school's basic rules. Some schools have no free-sparring rules or don't enforce the rules they have, and children have to depend on their partner to use control.

The instructor can explain to you the school's free-sparring rules and expectations of students during free-sparring.

What Type of Self-Defense Skills Are Taught?

Teaching self-defense skills must be done with the child's age, gender and needs in mind. It is thoughtless to teach self-defense techniques to seven or eight-year olds which are based on situations in which a 20-year old man might find himself.

☯ Discussing Scenarios

Students of all ages can use refresher courses on basic safety rules. Classes can present self-defense scenarios and allow children to practice different responses in a safe atmosphere. Scenarios can be based on real-life situations: a man asks for help finding his "lost" puppy; a car stops and the woman inside asks directions, offers candy, or tells the child his parents asked her to bring the child home.

Discussing these events in class, raising options and role-playing common sense ways to stay safe, reinforces the safety messages parents are trying to instill in their children. It also alerts children to different scenarios and types of tactics used by strangers to lure victims.

☯ Developing Self-Control and When to Use Skills

At recess, a group of children played King of the Mountain on a snow hill. A sixth-grader, taller and older than the first-graders playing the game, became overly aggressive, hitting and pushing them down. Another sixth-grader, who was studying martial arts, approached him, grabbed his hand in a finger lock and walked him down the snow mountain and to the teachers. Martial arts provided him with a safe, quiet, unobtrusive method of restraint.

Children are interested in learning to react to various school scenarios. Kindergartners and first-graders can learn how to escape from hand holds and arm grabs. As they grow older and more coordinated, they can be taught restraints. Knowing self-defense skills frees them from unwarranted worry and keeps them from resorting to whining or cowering from bullies which may only increase the abuse.

Through martial arts practice, children learn self-control. As they mature, grow stronger and older, and learn more difficult techniques, they should receive guidance on when to use their self-defense skills.

☯ Use of Forms

When faced with terrifying situations, people often report their minds going blank. They weren't prepared.

Forms, hyungs, poomse, sets and katas are names for the formalized patterns of movements taught in many of the martial arts. They give children a safe way to practice combinations, punches, and kicks, either by themselves or with others. Their hands, feet, and minds become so familiar with these movements they can respond instinctively in times of danger.

Studying the martial arts and enacting situations in the safety of class prepares children to keep their minds open and agile. They can more clearly evaluate what is happening and think of creative ways to react, take control and defuse situations.

☯ Importance of Shouting

Many martial arts styles teach shouts (called kiai or kihap). The shout begins in the lower abdomen, not in the throat. When the student exhales, the body's muscles tighten and energy is forced out. In addition to frightening opponents, the kihap helps students focus. Every shout in class contributes to children's confidence, to their abilities to stand-up to others and to stand-up for their own rights.

Young martial artists learn to display confidence, walk alertly and respond assertively. These actions can serve as protection against perpetrators from bullies in school to adults on the street who are looking for easy victims.

☯ Trusting Instincts

Children are encouraged in class to follow their instincts and to make their own safety a top priority. Repetition helps makes reactions and attitudes like awareness instinctive.

☯ Developing Awareness

Awareness, a sense of where they are and who is around them, is the key to personal safety for children. Classes often include simple exercises such as asking students to close their eyes and to describe the nearest exit in the room or the person behind them. These exercises help them learn the habit of noticing their surroundings.

☯ Reducing Anxiety

Studies have discovered that children who practice and develop self-defense skills have a lower level of anxiety. This shows in their confident walk, in their increased self-esteem, and in their common sense care for personal safety. Their status can change from one of potential victim to someone who is too much trouble to approach.

What Other Activities Are Offered?

Children in martial arts classes become part of a martial arts community and have many opportunities to practice their social skills and grow as martial artists.

☯ Demonstrations

Many schools take part in demonstrations for organizations such as the Scouts, for city festivals, for elementary and middle schools, etc. The demonstrations can be presented anyplace there is a stage or space for students to perform, including malls, auditoriums, arenas, and gymnasiums.

Some schools have students sign-up to participate when there is a demonstration scheduled. Other schools have regular demonstration teams, complete with identifying uniforms. As in schools with more loosely organized demonstration teams, students have regular practices, perform together, and develop camaraderie.

In addition to demonstrating their martial art's basics such as kicks and punches, the instructor can plan skits and routines based on the skills of the participants. Demonstrations are generally open to all students in the school, from the most experienced to the newest student.

Your child will be required to attend practices to prepare for each demonstration. Students are expected to be sharp, disciplined, respectful and able to accurately perform the routines. Not all students will participate in each activity.

☯ Competitions

Competitions offer many opportunities to develop friendships with students from across the state and country, especially for those students returning again and again to compete. Children also gain a great deal from watching others, learning their strengths, and sharing information.

☯ Summer Camps

Summer camps, whether church, YMCA, Boy Scout or Girl Scout, may offer special martial arts classes for children. These few hours during the week are geared toward basics, camaraderie and having fun. Many children have enrolled in martial arts schools after a week of summer camp lessons.

For more intensive training, there are specialized martial arts camps which bring in national experts. The camps focus their training on different ranks, e.g., a camp for black belts, red and brown belts, intermediate and so on. Specialized martial arts camps bring together dedicated students from a variety of schools and a wide geographical area.

☯ Workshops/Seminars

At times during your child's study, the instructor might bring in martial artists from another style to teach a workshop or seminar. For instance, a taekwondo or karate instructor might invite an aikido instructor to teach blending techniques. Students might be able to attend a workshop led by a martial artist of national renown. Or, the instructor can bring in fitness experts to discuss fitness and proper conditioning. Workshops and seminars can also teach forms, self-defense, and weapons. Based on the instructor's initiative or on input from parents, children can enjoy many opportunities, both formal and informal, to meet others and learn more about the martial arts.

☯ Parties

Schools may host Christmas and Halloween parties, family picnics and special weekend events. Children get to know instructors and other students in an atmosphere other than class. This helps them build a base of common experiences.

☯ Black Belt Clubs/Groups

Many times, schools sell memberships to black belt clubs. The clubs can go by a variety of names; whatever the instructor decides to call it. Benefits offered to black belt club members can include uniforms which are a different color from the rest of the students' uniforms or identifying patches on the uniforms. Memberships might enable these students to attend workshops or classes for free instead of the fee required by non-black belt club members. Specialized classes or workshops can include weapons classes, board-breaking sessions, forms and self-defense workshops, and fitness seminars. Some schools require students who want to become assistant instructors or instructors to belong to these clubs.

Other schools refuse to sell black belt clubs or to institute them. "Clubs tend to be exclusive rather than inclusive," an instructor of a large school said. "Our philosophy has always been that everyone respects each other regardless of belt or rank."

Instead, these schools have instituted informal groups called "Masters Group," "Instructors Group," "Black Belt Group," and "Color Belt Group." They hold informative meetings in which everyone discusses such topics as "How can we increase our quality?" and "What kinds of programs can we offer to enhance our school?"

There are no membership fees. "They are really a kind of forum and are not intended to separate one group from another," the instructor said.

This inclusive philosophy, committed to gathering input from all members, is practiced in many martial arts schools in Japan. "Black belts and instructors in Japan got together and discussed issues," said an instructor who had taught both in Japan and the United States.

(*Note*: Sometimes, it seems as if a Black Belt Club membership is really another term for long-term contract. As a parent of a youngster just starting out, don't be talked into buying this type of membership. You and your child need to discover if the martial arts classes are meeting your needs before you make a commitment.)

In Addition to Classes, Schools May Offer:

- ✓ Demonstrations
- ✓ A Demonstration Team
- ✓ Competitions
- ✓ Summer Camps
- ✓ Workshops
- ✓ Seminars with Guest Instructors
- ✓ Seminars about Health or Fitness
- ✓ Holiday Parties
- ✓ Birthday Parties
- ✓ Black Belt Clubs
- ✓ Specialized Skill Classes
- ✓ Leadership Clubs

Why are Terminology and History Taught?

Without history, terminology and philosophy, the study of the martial arts is relegated to sport. Martial arts is much more than a sporting activity.

"Without discipline, history, and the sense of respect linked to taekwondo, it loses context," said a taekwondo instructor. "Most schools train the mind as well as the body."

Children are practicing arts that have been modified over thousands of years. Arts reflect the experiences of thousands of men and women, evolving as countries' histories evolved. They incorporate attitudes of another country's culture. Children in classes are now part of martial arts' history and its future.

Each art has a philosophy for living, for behavior toward others, for teaching, and for facing challenges. Learning this philosophy enables students to adopt its attitudes in their daily lives, to improve their confidence and self-esteem, and to use the art's skills wisely.

Some modern schools teach martial arts techniques without the philosophical and historical background. This limits children's potential. Research studies have found children taking martial arts classes with history and philosophy incorporated into the lessons are less aggressive than those who study martial arts simply as a sport.

Where Can I Find Reference Materials?

Reference materials are available in libraries, martial arts magazines and catalogs, in book stores and on the internet (start at the martial arts library at http://www.turtlepress.com). They will help you help your child learn the material and provide you with background about the martial art your child is studying.

An instructor should be able to refer you to reference books he or she uses for teaching and suggest resource materials. The instructor who creates guidelines of what is expected at each rank contributes to your child's ease of learning and to your ability to help your child study. Some schools create their own lending library of supplemental, age-appropriate materials. Other schools sell reference materials, and most schools carry martial arts catalogs.

What is the Class Schedule?

The weekly schedule (the days the school is open or closed) is not consistent among all martial arts schools. Often the schedule is arranged around the instructor's other job, since he or she may hold a job in addition to running a martial arts school. The instructor should be able to give you a copy of the class schedule.

☆ Class Length

Class length can vary depending on the ages and abilities of the children, or each class can be the same amount of time regardless of the students' ages or ranks. It is up to the instructor to establish how long classes will be.

On average, children ages four and five can usually handle a class of 30 minutes which expands to 45 minutes or so when they reach the ages of six and seven. Classes lasting 50 to 60 minutes are possible for those older than seven. Children who are thirteen years and older can handle 60 to 90 minute classes.

☆ Class Groupings

Classes may be open to students of any age or rank, or classes may be divided according to age groups and ranks. Many beginner students can take at least two classes per week and should do so if at all possible. As they progress through the ranks, they will want to take three, or sometimes more, lessons a week.

☆ Open Class Times

Open class times can be wonderful opportunities for children to ask for specialized help and work on various aspects of the art. If open class times are regularly scheduled, it can be extremely helpful if higher ranked class members take part of the time to seek out lower belts and work with them. If a regular class has been turned into an open class, the instructor might designate someone to work with the younger children or lower ranked students. Hopefully, the school has established an atmosphere which encourages children to ask upper belts for assistance.

☆ Arrival Time

Arrival at the school should be timed so children can change into their uniforms (if they aren't already wearing them), warm-up, and talk with their friends before class. This helps them approach class relaxed and ready to learn. When they are younger, this attitude helps them focus on the class, until they develop the ability to put the outside world aside while they are in class.

☆ Late!

Each school sets its own policy for late arrivals. If children are late, regardless of the reason, they may be asked to do a few push-ups before joining class and standing at the end of the line. Children are told to stand at the end of the line rather than their usual spot (which can be based on rank) because it is less disruptive to the class.

☆ Workshops and Seminars

Workshops and seminars are often longer than the school's usual class length since they have a particular focus. They can be held in addition to regular classes, or be scheduled during a regular class time. Each instructor develops his or her own philosophy regarding the timing of workshops and seminars.

What Is the Structure of a Normal Class?

Class structure varies, depending on the martial art and the teacher. Classes should start with warm-ups and stretches to loosen muscles and prepare the body for fast movements. Then the instructor will introduce new skills and give students time to practice them. Rest periods occur informally when students observe how a technique is done and listen to the instructor. Some martial arts classes include time for meditation. At the end of each class, students should do cool down movements to help them recover from the workout and remain flexible.

While class is in session, the instructor may help familiarize students with terminology by giving commands and counting in the language of the country from which the martial arts originated. The instructor may also include bits of history and philosophy, explanations of techniques and ask questions of the students.

What Is My Child Required to Have for Class?

☯ Uniforms

Uniforms fit loosely, allowing students to move freely. The uniform and white belt are sometimes included in an introductory trial offer package. Uniforms and the belts which designate ranks are meant to be worn proudly, but humbly. Students' goals are to learn the requirements of their rank so they can test for the next belt rank and for the opportunity to learn more.

Students attending classes held at the Y, a college, or through a city's recreation system may substitute loose fitting clothing for uniforms. Similarly, when you take advantage of free trial lessons, your child can wear loose clothing.

☯ Free-Sparring Equipment

Equipment needed for classes depends on the art and the teacher. For example, sparring equipment at some schools consists of headgear, footgear and gloves while at others it consists of headgear, gloves, shin pads, and rib padding. Some schools allow students to free-spar at the white belt level, while other schools won't allow students to begin free-sparring until they've reached a higher rank. Some leave the decision of when to start free-sparring up to the student.

Ask the instructor the cost of the required sparring equipment and when you will have to purchase it. Instructors can be helpful in selecting the proper size gear for your child. Many instructors will order equipment from catalogs while others have an equipment store or pro shop on the premises. You might run across an instructor who prefers you order through the school rather than on your own through the catalogs.

Sometimes the instructor sells used equipment that other students have traded in for larger sizes. Or, the instructor will supply equipment which students share when it comes time for the free-sparring section of class.

Other options for finding the proper equipment are open to you. You may connect with a parent in your school who is trying to sell his or her child's good, used equipment. A secondhand, sporting goods store might carry used and sometimes new equipment at a savings. Depending on the current inventory, you might find almost everything you need. Be sure you only purchase free-sparring gear that is in excellent condition. For safety, protective equipment must not be ripped or excessively worn.

☯ Personal Hygiene

Keeping fingernails and toenails clipped short decreases the chance of injury. In addition, every student must remove all jewelry so it can't be broken or harm others during class.

Each student's uniform should be kept clean and worn proudly. For youngsters, this means making sure they do not wear their uniforms out to play after class or to the dinner table. While your child may want to wear his new uniform day and night, it will last much longer if you insist it be worn only for classes and other martial arts events.

☯ Attitude

Children's attitudes toward class have an enormous effect on whether they succeed. Students must bring a desire to learn to class. This attitude opens them up to new ideas, new movements and new skills. If they don't want to be there, their negative attitude can affect other students' behaviors and enjoyment of class. Students' willingness to listen, learn and try new things helps them to concentrate, respond and follow directions to the best of their abilities.

Real Life Profile

Marilyn Lee

A Deep Love for the Arts

Marilyn Lee loved watching her grandmother's Chinese kung-fu movies. "It looked like a dance. Ever since I can remember, I wanted to be in the martial arts and have a cool samurai hair-do," she said.

At five and six-years old, she would dress in clothes that looked like the clothing worn in the movies. "I wore a bathrobe and walked around with a tree branch as my make-believe sword."

Her father enrolled her in a taekwondo school when she was seven-years old. At that time, she was the youngest person there and one of few female students. "I was also short for my age," she said.

Her free-sparring partners were older and taller than herself. "Sometimes I felt the guys regarded me with the attitude, 'She's just a girl.' The boys were afraid to hit me. So I received patronizing taps for punches," she said. At first, she felt intimidated, but then she began viewing free-sparring the boys as a challenge and looked forward to it.

"The adult males didn't look down at me or fight down to me. Eventually, I gained respect. I conquered my fears of fighting people older and bigger than me, and felt like one of the group," she said.

Her first school emphasized discipline, proper techniques and forms. "I felt it laid a groundwork for me to build upon," she said. "At this point, I no longer feared competing against people bigger than me."

After several years at that studio and some time spent not studying the arts, Marilyn enrolled in another studio.

For the first week, Marilyn was pleased with her new studio and new Asian master instructor. "He gave a huge speech about how he learned the art in Korea. I assumed his technique would be better, and he would teach discipline at a higher level. After a week, I was appalled at how the children (students) just ran around during class. The dojo was just a playground."

As Marilyn rose through the ranks at the second school, more and more children her age enrolled. "At first, I didn't think much about it," she said. "Then I thought, 'Oh good, I have playmates.' But they didn't listen to him, so they didn't learn anything. Then I thought about how easy it would be to fight kids my own age. Eventually, I looked to the older people to help me out rather than the other kids. The older students gave me more of a challenge."

The second studio emphasized fighting. "They taught efficient and fast fighting techniques. I felt we were pretty good. But when we competed at tournaments, I saw we were not as good. I realized that the techniques I learned were based on strength which doesn't always suit everyone. We weren't taught how to fight strategically."

Ultimately, her long-held views on the martial arts differed from the instructor. "He felt the martial art was more of a sport," Marilyn said. "Taekwondo is more than a fighting art. It lays the foundation for developing instincts for something more."

After classes, Marilyn said she felt very confident and able to handle herself in different situations as well as physically fit. "But," she said, "I still felt incomplete because I never mastered the art to my satisfaction and so never went on to black belt. I feel I am not worthy of that rank."

Marilyn injured her knee while playing on the high school tennis team and stopped taking taekwondo. "When it heals, I might like to take the martial arts again," she said.

"I grew up loving the martial arts. I never grew up loving track and field, soccer, and volleyball. They grew on me. It all has to do with what we enjoy doing, what we really love and find passion in doing," she said.

7

How to Evaluate a Trial Lesson

Most schools offer trial lessons so students can base their decision to join on actual class experiences. Your child should take this lesson in the same class he or she will enter as an enrolled student. It helps to go beyond asking: "Did you like it?" and evaluate the lesson based on the points that follow.

Sometimes, schools give a private lesson as a trial to potential new students. The close attention is wonderful, and children can receive good teaching. But since regular classes aren't taught this way, the private trial lesson is misleading. Some schools start all enrolled, beginning students with a few private or semi-private lessons in order to prepare them for their first group class. This is different from private trial lessons.

☆ Skill/Knowledge Levels

Ideally, students wearing belts of the same color display the same skills and knowledge and differ from students of other belt ranks. For example, blue belts as a whole are not as skilled as brown belts or others of a higher rank, and the blue belts' techniques are more difficult than those performed by lower ranking students. Allow some variation due to each child's abilities, learning styles, and commitment to practice. And, of course, the instructor's knowledge and skill level should be greater than the students.

☆ Teaching Methods

Class should consist of more than one method to present and teach the material. Large and small group exercises offer a number of ways to creatively teach and practice a skill.

Sometimes a class is structured so it is entirely a large group exercise, consisting of a variety of activities. For instance, children might practice blocks by themselves while facing the front of the room, practice blocks while facing another student who is also blocking at the same time, practice blocks while moving across the floor, practice blocks in combinations with other techniques, and practice blocking techniques thrown by partners.

Many times, the instructor divides each belt level into smaller groups so they can receive closer instruction from an assistant instructor or a higher ranked belt.

☆ Respect

Each person in class has value and that value must be encouraged to grow. Your child's growth in the martial arts or as a person can be affected by the amount of respect shown by the instructor. Students who feel respected respond confidently. Listen to the instructor's tone of voice as well as what is said to the students. If the instructor addresses each student by name, it is a formal recognition of the importance of that child.

Students are to treat instructors with respect. This is not the "you-are-an-adult,-you-can-do-no-wrong" respect. Nor is it military-style respect. Appropriate respect honors the knowledge of the instructor. Students refer to the instructor as Mr., Mrs., Ms., Ma'am, Sir, Sensei, Sempei, Sabumnim, or whatever the tradition is at the school.

Students may formally address black belts as Sir or Ma'am, Mr. or Mrs. Students at the same belt rank below black belt greet each other and students of lower rank by their first names.

All students should be treated respectfully regardless of age and gender. It is up to each student to help make it a successful experience for other students.

What Does a Good Class Consist Of?

Classes for beginning students should be available two to three times a week. But even if more classes are open to beginners, children should limit weekly class attendance to these visits. In the early stages, there's a danger of burn-out if children attend every day.

☆ Warm-Ups

A good class starts with warm-ups and stretching exercises. Many students stretch before class actually starts, but not everyone does this. Taking a few minutes at the beginning of class provides everyone with a consistent set of exercises to prepare their bodies for the workout. Their bodies become conditioned. Once they learn the routine, they can run through the exercises whenever and wherever they practice. During the beginning sets of exercises, students become familiar with reacting to counts and instructions.

☆ Class Focus/Teaching Methods

Classes generally focus on one or more aspects of the martial art such as self-defense, defensive and offensive movements, restraints, breathing, balance, focus, forms, kicks, linear and circular movements. The instructor implements activities which help teach the aspect of the art the class is focusing on and reviews new skills. Students practice as a group, by themselves, or with partners.

An instructor who uses innovative and varied teaching methods keeps the class flowing and interesting. Since people learn differently, using a variety of activities to teach a concept or action increases the likelihood of the material being learned. Variety makes repetition more exciting and decreases boredom.

Practice sessions can consist of group led activities in which the instructor asks a group within the class to contribute something to the entire class, i.e., demonstrate a form or a particular combination of techniques. Or individual students can be asked to demonstrate and explain certain skills. This allows people with different strengths to lead sections of the class and learn to give instructions in a manner that others can understand.

During classes, there are times when individuals work by themselves to improve techniques. The entire class is given the same overall direction, but each student decides what to practice within those guidelines. For instance, students instructed to practice offensive techniques select which ones they will work on.

Often, the instructor tells the entire group specifically what to do or breaks them up into smaller groups for small group activities. Students of higher belt ranks can be selected to work with the lower ranking students, teaching forms, step-sparring, self-defense, etc.

Children partner for activities which are best learned in twos. Working in pairs gives children the chance to work with others who are taller, stronger, or smaller than they are. They learn which techniques work on different sizes of people. They may also practice terminology and answer questions one-on-one.

The teacher may ask questions during class or pass along stories which demonstrate the art's basic philosophy.

☆ Cool-Down

At the end of each class, students will perform a few cool-down movements. Depending on the martial arts style, meditation and quiet time will be included in every class or only when it is appropriate for the class focus.

A good school will not emphasize just one of these class elements but provide a solid mix. While each class has a focus, such as breathing or balance, many elements of the art will be covered during each class because the whole is improved when details are improved.

Since some class activities are more physically demanding than others, students need adequate recovery time. Instructors should intersperse physical activities with mentally challenging ones or with less physically demanding activities.

☆ Learning Atmosphere

Children learn best in a positive learning atmosphere. Good instructors establish the type of atmosphere in which critiques, rather than criticism, are provided. If children are overly concerned with perfection and with not making a mistake, they won't keep trying new things. They will never grow in the art.

☆ Self-Control/Discipline

Students must practice self-control and discipline. When students act up, they distract other students and interfere with their learning and class time. Someone could get hurt because a few students are not paying attention.

"I really need the students to pay attention and follow me," said an instructor. "So if someone isn't, I ask them to sit out and watch class. But I have them sit out in a spot where they can join in when they are ready."

☆ Free-Sparring/Partner Safety

Safety should be emphasized during free-sparring bouts as well as anytime a student works with a partner. The instructor usually reminds students of the school's safety rules before these activities.

Free-sparring rules describe the amount of contact: such as none, low or medium, as well as a reminder of which parts of the body can or cannot be hit. When working with a partner, students are reminded to tell the other student in advance if they plan a take-down or to support their partner during throws.

Schools which emphasize fighting might not have rules or enforce the ones they have. This can cause problems for students enrolled in fighting schools.

"A lot of people used free-sparring as a power trip," said a student from a school with no free-sparring rules. "They didn't care if they hurt someone. Some people used common sense, but others were out for blood."

When students from these schools transfer into schools with a different focus, it can cause short-term problems while they learn to adjust their fighting style. The instructor should be aware of the situation and help the new student adjust it.

Children cannot assume that because people are older or because they are upper belts they will look out for the younger, more inexperienced student. "White belts didn't know what to expect from upper belts," the student added. "They'd just hope the upper belt was nice."

At the same time, it is often the lower belt with little control who can easily get carried away during sparring. Free-sparring rules protect them and their partners as they learn control, techniques, and timing.

What Type of Skills Will Be Taught In a Good Class?

A good class teaches many basic skills, while emphasizing one or two. The following is a list of basic skills to look for when evaluating children's trial lessons.

☯ Self-Defense

Self-defense cannot be taught in just one class, whether one hour or three hours long. It takes repetition to internalize awareness and movements. A few minutes of instruction in each class emphasizes the importance of self-defense, teaches new movements, lets students practice ones they already know, and reminds them of the need to be aware. Often schools supplement classes with special seminars or workshops focusing exclusively on self-defense.

☯ Offensive Skills

Offensive skills (punching, striking, kicking) can be performed with the hands and the feet. When teaching offensive skills, instructors emphasize combinations and correctly performed techniques. They explain where and when to use the skills and their purposes.

☯ Defensive Skills

Blocks should be performed as well as offensive skills, since effective blocks can end an attack. These skills can be practiced individually or in combinations, with or without partners, while moving across the floor, or while standing still.

☯ Sparring/Weapons Practice

Not all martial arts teach sparring or weapons. For instance, aikido doesn't include sparring in its philosophy; only an offshoot of aikido teaches sparring. Aikido does teach weapons such as the jo through formalized katas.

Some schools teach weapons in specialized classes after children reach a certain age or level of competency. Instructors may work privately with a few students on such advanced skills.

Sparring skills develop confidence and awareness. Children learn to observe many things such as their partner's movements in order to predict the next attack, their partner's fighting style, and where openings are. Children learn to react automatically.

Some schools offer sparring classes dedicated to teaching competitive sparring, and other schools will work individually with their students who want to improve their competitive sparring skills.

☯ Forms

Many martial arts teach formalized sets of movements (called forms, sets, hyung, poomse or kata) which allow students to practice techniques by themselves or with a group. Students become used to performing blocks and attacks individually and in combinations. Basic skills are improved as students perfect their forms. Forms may also provide students with history lessons, since some are named for a person or event.

☯ Fitness/Conditioning

Many of the techniques taught in martial arts classes require a certain level of fitness and conditioning. Muscles must be prepared for rapid movements; the body must be in condition to perform techniques which become more demanding as the student advances in the arts. Conditioning exercises include warm-ups, stretches, balance, strength, and endurance.

In addition to exercises performed as a group in class, students, especially those interested in competition, can work with the instructor on appropriate conditioning training outside of class to improve their endurance, strength and flexibility.

Those who practice intensively two to three times a week will improve their overall fitness level. Some schools provide fitness equipment to help strengthen the body and increase flexibility. This equipment shouldn't be used by young children.

☯ Concentration/Focus

These skills are included in every aspect of the martial arts. Students focus and concentrate on what they are doing, on the instructor, and on their partners. When they perform self-defense and sparring skills, they learn to react automatically and use the correct technique and action for the situation.

☯ Social Skills

If given opportunities, children learn how to interact appropriately with others, regardless of their ages. Planned interactions during classes can encourage and teach proper behavior.

☯ Proper Breathing

Breathing supplies oxygen to all parts of the body, keeping the extremities loose and ready for action. Breathing properly is calming and helps keep a person alert. When children breathe correctly, they perform forms, exercises, and techniques without losing energy.

☯ Balance

Proper balance is necessary in the martial arts. Many times, students find themselves lying on the ground because they weren't balanced properly. Students improve balance while performing forms and techniques. Special exercises such as doing techniques or forms with their eyes closed can help them work on their balance.

Elements of a Well Rounded Curriculum:

✓ Self-Defense

✓ Offensive Skills

✓ Defensive Skills

✓ Sparring Skills

✓ Weapons (optional)

✓ Forms, Hyungs, Kata

✓ Fitness

✓ Conditioning

✓ Concentration

✓ Focus

✓ Social Skills

✓ Proper Breathing

✓ Balance

Is This Class Right for My Child?

Classes should be designed to fulfill children's needs, not the needs and expectations of the instructors.

Your child should come out of the class feeling positive about the lesson, the teacher, and the overall experience. Ask your child questions such as: "Did you have fun?" "Did you like it?" "What did you learn?"

Children get very excited about learning and demonstrating skills they feel are within the reach of their capabilities.

Children can study with adults, but it is more fun for them if classes consist of a mixture of ages and sizes. They make new friends and practice with students their own size.

If this is your child's first class, he or she is going to be excited. But how are other students reacting? If other students leave class feeling excited, pumped up, and laughing, the instructor is working hard to create a positive atmosphere and is probably using a variety of activities to teach and reinforce a skill so children continue to have fun in the lessons.

8

Evaluating An Instructor

Choosing the best school includes selecting the best, most ethical instructor since children will emulate this person. In the movie, *Karate Kid*, the students of the bullying instructor adopted his attitude and ethics. This holds true in everyday life. You will often find children who mimic the actions and attitude of adults they respect and look up to. As parents of young children, in addition to hoping our children find good role models, we can guide them toward people we feel will provide good role modeling.

By observing how students, assistant instructors, and instructors behave toward others in the class and in the waiting room, you will begin to understand the attitude which has been adopted by the school. One mother expressed amazement at the friendliness of the black belts as they walked through the waiting room and talked with her six-year old daughter while she waited for her older brother to finish class.

Other parents' interests in the activities of the students taking lessons as well as their younger brothers and sisters can also reflect the school's attitude as established by the instructor. An overall atmosphere of friendliness and support creates a community in which your child will want to spend time. This atmosphere contributes to his or her success.

The instructor must be mature. Not necessarily old, but able to place what is right for the child above the instructor's personal goals. An instructor who is secure in his or her accomplishments and capabilities will not spend time bad-mouthing other schools and instructors or competing with students.

The instructor's goal should be to help children grow to the best of their abilities. Some students will ultimately surpass the instructor. If the instructor is mature and professional, this growth will please, not intimidate him or her.

The instructor who can clearly state objectives for the class and individual students, can develop curriculum and use innovative teaching methods will enhance your child's knowledge and martial arts capabilities.

Does the Instructor Communicate Well With Your Child?

Students will approach an instructor who is open to talking with them and who they believe is interested in helping them improve. They will often avoid an instructor who acts superior and unapproachable; an instructor whose attitude effectively cuts off communication.

Children relate to the instructor who speaks to them without patronizing or making fun of them. "Communication between a student and an instructor is most important," a taekwondo instructor said. "You must communicate at their level and remember that all students are at different levels."

The instructor should speak clearly with a firm, not intimidating, tone of voice. The instructor must retain authority while cultivating friendly, supportive relationships with students. If students know the instructor is in control, they relax, enjoy class and learn.

The information should also be concise and relevant. If the instructor rambles, children's concentration will ramble.

Does the Instructor Know How to Provide Constructive Feedback?

Constructive criticism helps children improve. It includes positive comments about what they are doing well, points out skills needing improvement and explains what to do to improve these skills.

If an instructor is negative and constantly criticizes the students, they will become nervous wrecks, more concerned with not upsetting the instructor than with learning the material.

At the same time, if the instructor does not correct students, but continuously tells them they are doing fine, the children will never learn. They will have no idea what needs improving. Often, children interpret this as meaning the instructor doesn't believe they can improve. Children want to believe the instructor cares and believes in them, and they work harder for an instructor who does.

It takes more effort on the instructor's part to set expectations, develop appropriate teaching methods, and expect require children to achieve them, than it does to decide it is impossible to explain things to children.

Once the instructor's expectations are lowered, children's expectations of themselves are lowered. One martial arts school which changed its requirements over the years discovered this to be true. In the beginning, children were expected to memorize the same definitions as adults. Children rose to the occasion. Then it was decided children shouldn't be required to do this. The instructor, judges, parents and the children expected, accepted and received a lower standard of performance overall.

Does the Instructor Teach Class Regularly?

As an instructor and school gain in popularity, the instructor sometimes teaches less. This can be a real loss. Look for an instructor who teaches, is willing to demonstrate his or her skills during class as well as spend time with your child, helping the child improve, talking with and answering the child's questions before or after class. Active instructors are often more enthusiastic about their art, about teaching, and about the accomplishments and lives of their students.

Does the Instructor Encourage Student Growth?

Instructors expect beginning students to practice only what they are learning in class. This could entail practicing one stance or a punch. In this stage of their study, instructors are concerned children will practice and reinforce the wrong techniques. As students advance, instructors will suggest students practice their forms, memorization, basic drills and other activities which can be done by themselves outside of class. This enables children to take responsibility for their own growth and advancement in the arts.

What is the Teacher's Teaching Style?

Today's children have grown up viewing fast-paced, interactive learning methods on television. Old style lectures and endless repetition quickly deflate their interests. An instructor who continues to study, who investigates and uses innovative teaching methods which offer fun and exciting twists to repetitive class activities, will keep children involved. An enthusiastic instructor is committed to teaching children.

Instructors who alter their teaching styles to fit the learning styles of all children in class will enable more children to successfully learn the martial arts. When a variety of methods are used, it reinforces the material, increasing children's chances of learning.

Children respond well to lessons which are fun and taught in a creative, interactive way. It requires much effort, patience, ingenuity, and willingness to look at and try alternative teaching styles. Some instructors are naturals; many more are not. But if the desire and enthusiasm are present, instructors will succeed in reaching children.

Can the Instructor Adapt to Changing Class Conditions?

Sometimes classes flow and everybody is in sync. Nothing can go wrong. Other times, a young child might refuse to come to class. Another might be distracted by all the activity and not listen to the instructor. When most of the class appears lethargic or overly energetic, a good instructor accepts the class plan is not working, alters it to take advantage of the situation, and regains children's attention.

No classroom situation is perfect. Nor are all children at the same physical development level. Some are exceptionally gifted and athletic. Others are clumsy and uncoordinated. All can succeed at martial arts. However, some will take longer to learn. The instructor should not concentrate on one group over the other, but give attention to all groups.

Can the Instructor Skillfully Teach Mixed Age Classes?

As children advance through the ranks, they will take classes with adults. Children should not be catered to in these situations or ignored. They are expected to participate to the best of their abilities because at each belt rank, they need to know the same information and demonstrate the same skills as adults. Mixed classes give children opportunities to try out techniques with people of many sizes and to interact with adults.

Does the Instructor Effectively Discipline Rule Breakers?

An instructor expects children to behave. Rules are stated and are expected to be followed. The facility is used by all and everyone is responsible for using it properly. Each person is responsible to help classes go well, not just the instructor. Sometimes, people don't understand this.

When bad behavior occurs, the instructor should promptly enforce the rules. A good instructor is prepared with alternative plans to encourage all children to participate well in class. Find out what methods the instructor prefers to use when disciplining students. What may sound like a reasonable idea to one person, might appall another.

Some instructors demand respect just because they are instructors. True respect develops for those instructors who earn it, by their ethics and attitude, by their knowledge and enthusiastic approach to teaching and life, by their willingness to teach and help, and by their willingness to learn from their students.

Does the Instructor Break Down Complex Skills?

An effective way to teach children is the building block method which takes a basic skill and expands upon it. With the building block method, martial arts instructors break techniques into smaller, manageable steps. Once children know how to perform the techniques, others are added, and soon children are learning intricate skills and combinations. This method works best if instructors both describe and demonstrate the steps.

When teaching forms, instructors emphasize the overall appearance and then work on the specific details which make up the whole, focusing on the correct performance of each step. This enables students to develop good habits early in the learning process so they don't have to waste time unlearning bad habits.

Does the Instructor Maintain a Professional Demeanor?

The level of professionalism displayed by the instructor and staff will affect children's study of the martial arts.

An instructor who has to prove he or she is better than one of the students is unprofessional. There is no professional reason an instructor has to defeat or humiliate a student in class.

Bad mouthing the competition, whether in private or in front of a class, is an example of an insecure, unprofessional instructor.

A parent, whose daughter and brother were in the martial arts for many years, described his first visit with an established instructor. "I'd heard he was knowledgeable and had experience. In our meeting, he talked a lot about how good or bad other schools were and that he was the only true martial artist in town."

An instructor disadvantages current students when he or she leaves a class to talk to potential new students. At a professional school, another black belt takes over the class, students practice independently or in groups, or an office manager discusses most of the details with the prospective student until the instructor is free. At an unprofessional school, students wait in their lines—doing nothing—until the instructor returns.

Personal attention is gratifying to new students. But next time, it could be your child left standing in the class.

Unethical, unprofessional people exist in every profession including the martial arts. There are unscrupulous instructors and students who don't live out the arts' moral philosophy, who abuse their positions of authority and take advantage of or harass students.

Whether the harassment takes the form of physical, sexual or verbal abuse, it is not appropriate. Sexual harassment or abuse must be reported immediately to the authorities. Non-criminal verbal or emotional abuse needs to be confronted directly with the people involved and the instructor should be informed. If he or she does nothing or is the one abusing power, the student should find another school. If the school is associated with an affiliate organization, file a report on the behavior and situation. A complaint can also be filed with the Better Business Bureau or the state agency that licenses schools.

Is the Instructor Open to Input?

A professional instructor will talk with parents and with families, listening and responding to their questions and complaints. Some suggestions are valid and should be seriously considered; others are not. Open communication in which parental input is seriously considered can help the instructor differentiate between the two and make improvements.

Children meet many challenges in their daily lives. Studying the martial arts can be a positive, esteem-building experience if it is learned at the right school with a professional, enthusiastic instructor.

Does the Instructor Help Students Maintain a Positive Training Philosophy?

Starting with the basics, training builds into a complete program which helps students learn and work to the best of their capabilities. With each success comes the right to learn the next step and reach for further success. The curriculum is established by the martial art and taught by the instructor.

In academic schools, teachers develop lesson plans to teach the curriculum, rather than teaching with an erratic, hit or miss approach. Their daily lesson plans help children reach the goals established by the educational system. Each day's work builds upon the success of the prior day's work, until the entire subject is taught.

No less should be expected from martial arts instructors who plan classes to teach the martial arts curriculum. This is a basic educational philosophy—true no matter what the subject.

Many schools provide written guidelines which clearly state what students will learn at each belt level. In addition to physical skills and techniques, these guidelines can cover such things as terminology, philosophy and historical knowledge. They can also include the emotional responses and social skills expected of students as they progress through the levels.

These guidelines can help determine the instructor's professionalism, enthusiasm, organization and commitment to teaching. They are a tangible, positive record of what your child has learned at each rank. They also are one of the tools you, your child and instructor can use to determine if your child is ready for promotion.

Is the Instructor Skilled in the Martial Arts?

Just because a person opens a martial arts school does not mean he or she is skilled. There are cases in which first degree black belts open schools and suddenly are sporting second degree black belts - just a few months after attaining the first degree. There is no recognized licensing or certifying body for instructors. While there are many private certifications available, they are no guarantee of an instructor's ability to teach.

Ask questions regarding how long the instructor has trained as well as the kinds, places, and length of specialized training workshops. Find out how many years of experience the instructor has as a teacher of the martial arts and where this experience took place.

Another indicator of an instructor's skill is the number of upper rank and black belt students in classes. Advanced students stay in and attend schools in which the instructor continues to challenge them to grow and improve.

Is the Instructor Fit?

It's not uncommon to find instructors who are no longer physically fit. Since they are teaching and acting as role models, instructors can be expected to maintain their own overall fitness and healthy lifestyles, allowing some leeway for their bodies to reflect their age.

Instructor Evaluation Checklist:

1. Is the atmosphere in the school one that appeals to you?	yes	no
2. Is the instructor mature?	yes	no
3. Does the instructor have clear goals for his or her students?	yes	no
4. Does the instructor communicate well with your child?	yes	no
5. Does the instructor provide constructive feedback?	yes	no
6. Does the instructor teach class regularly?	yes	no
7. Does the instructor encourage student growth?	yes	no
8. Is the instructor's teaching style suitable for your child?	yes	no
9. Can the instructor adapt to changing class situations?	yes	no
10. Can the instructor skillfully teach mixed age classes?	yes	no
11. Does the instructor effectively discipline rule-breakers?	yes	no
12. Does the instructor break down complex skills?	yes	no
13. Does the instructor maintain a professional demeanor?	yes	no
14. Is the instructor open to input?	yes	no
15. Does the instructor encourage a positive training attitude?	yes	no
16. Is the instructor skilled in the martial arts?	yes	no
17. Is the instructor fit?	yes	no

Total "yes" answers: _____

Total "no" answers: _____

An instructor that is right for your child will have at least 10 "yes" answers on the above checklist. If you have less than 10 "yes" answers, keep looking for the right instructor. If you had difficulty answering all of the questions, you may need to meet with the instructor again or watch another class to get a more complete impression of the instructor's skills and teaching style.

9

Evaluating Fees and Contracts

Each school establishes its own fees and payment schedules unless it is part of a chain. Even then, fees may be adjusted to reflect the area's cost of living.

Over the years, as the popularity of the martial arts has increased, more schools have opened and martial arts has become a business. Consequently, instructors entered the field who were often more concerned with making money than with teaching the art.

Traditionally, students paid by the month. They didn't purchase or sign long-term contracts. A few schools still follow this month-by-month policy. Many schools require a student to sign a longer term contract.

The challenge to today's dedicated martial arts instructor is to focus on teaching the martial arts while running the school as a successful business. Business is not an evil word. A successful business has to be able to pay for the building, maintenance, utilities, insurance and associated expenses. A strong desire to teach the martial arts provides a reason for the instructor's business, and a well-run business gives the instructor the freedom to continue teaching the martial arts.

A school which combines business and education in an ethical manner is mutually beneficial to students and instructor.

What Length of Commitment Is Required?

Contracts can be monthly, quarterly, yearly or longer. Schools often require payment in full for contracts of a shorter length or establish monthly installments for longer term commitments. Some charge per lesson rather than per month.

Other schools sell contracts based on belt ranks. For instance, if the goal is to obtain the level of brown belt, the contract will cost "x" amount of money. When it comes time to renew, students sign another contract which promises they will reach a higher level. Payment for these contracts can be due immediately, monthly, or in whatever manner has been established by the school.

Recreation programs offered by cities, colleges and universities, or clubs such as the YMCA, may sign students up for six weeks, a semester, or a summer program. These programs are paid for at registration.

If possible, select a school which is sensitive to the issues faced by parents of young children. Some schools will not sign children up for longer than a three month contract. The instructors are aware that children's interests ebb and flow, and the instructors do not want to burden parents with long-term contracts and years of financial commitment if their children are no longer taking classes.

How Are Payments Collected?

Many instructors hire independent contractors or companies to bill and collect payments while others handle this part of the business themselves. Those who use a billing service find it beneficial to their relationships with students. The service is responsible for keeping track of payments and contacting students, and according to whatever agreement they've signed, might not inform the instructor until the student's bill is past 60 days. There is no build-up of animosity in the interim. Upon notification, the instructor can talk with the students or their families and renegotiate the payment so students can pay all of their fees.

Billing companies encourage the use of electronic payments as convenient methods for both instructor and student. Many instructors are switching to this method to save time and money.

Instructors who are directly involved in collecting money find that much of their time is spent dealing with business/clerical issues rather than teaching. If the instructor has hired permanent clerical help or uses another form of billing, it could indicate the instructor's priority is teaching.

What Type of Contract Is Used?

Contracts are binding agreements. Take time to review the contract or agreement before you sign it. You can even take it home or show it to your lawyer if you have questions. Here are a few items that may be included in a contract over and above the cost of lessons:

$ Initiation Fees

Some schools institute an initiation fee to cover paperwork such as registering the student, billing, and contract work. Ask if this a "one-time only" fee.

$ Membership Dues

Membership dues may be renewed every year and are in addition to your monthly payment. They can be used to cover the office's paperwork, billing procedures, facility maintenance, health club fees, etc.

$ Registration Fees

This is another version of the initiation fee. It might be charged for registering a new pupil either with the school or with the parent chain.

$ Association Membership Fees

If a school belongs to an association (and there are a number of them in existence), students can be required to pay a fee to the parent organization. Sometimes this is included in the fees paid to the school.

$ Promotion Fees

Most schools charge a promotion fee each time children test to a new level. These fees are established by the instructor and differ from school to school. Generally, promotion fees are the same for lower ranks but rise as students reach more advanced levels.

$ Add-ons

Some schools offer and charge for specialized classes in such skills as sparring, self-defense, board-breaking and weapons. Private lessons can add another fee onto the basic cost. Students might have to sign-up to use specialized equipment, such as weights and fitness machines.

$ Down Payment

If there is a down payment, find out what it covers. Is it part of the total cost of the lessons and subtracted from the entire amount, or is it an amount that covers registration?

$ Late Fees

Ask whether the school has a grace period. Some schools charge a late fee which goes into effect the first day a payment is late.

$ Finance Charges

Some schools include a finance charge if the full amount of the contract/agreement is not immediately paid.

$ Reciprocal Benefits

Schools belonging to a chain might be able to offer the opportunity for children to attend another school in the same chain at no additional charge. Others will allow for trading of teachers, but not of students, because each school is individually owned and run.

$ Transfer/Freeze Privileges

When the instructor verbally promises or suggests the capability of transferring your contract to another school or even to a new student, read the contract. Is it in writing? Does it list the reciprocal schools? Is transferring memberships a benefit found in the school because it belongs to a chain? Has anyone ever successfully sold or transferred their contract to another student or to another school either in or out of a chain? Are there limitations on who memberships may be sold to (i.e. new members only)?

$ Required Equipment and Uniforms

Each school decides what color and type of uniform its students will wear. It also establishes rules for sparring equipment including at what level students will start to use it. You might not have to order sparring equipment right away.

When purchased through the school, the cost of the first uniform can be included in special introductory offers, paid for upon delivery, or spread over the year in monthly payments. Uniforms can also be purchased through catalogs. Does the school require students to have identifying patches or embroidery on their uniforms? If so, find out how much they cost and if everything is available to you through the school. Sometimes the school's logo, patches, etc. must be on the uniform by the time students test for a certain rank. If so, which rank is this?

Families benefit when schools sell used uniforms and sparring equipment or supply sparring equipment which is shared by students in class.

$ Liability

Well-run schools rarely have accidents because they establish and enforce safety rules. Make sure the school has insurance coverage and find out what it covers. In addition, parents should carry their own medical coverage.

$ Limitations

As beginning students, especially those who sign-up under special introductory promotions, children could be limited to a certain number of lessons each week. Some schools might offer only two children's beginning classes per week under the special promotion. Many schools publish class schedules identifying which classes are open to children, adults, mixed ranks, beginning ranks and advanced ranks. Students can only attend those classes which are tailored to their rank.

$ Competitions/Class Requirements Which Cost Extra

The instructor should be able to tell you (hopefully in writing) how many classes your child must attend before testing for the next rank. There is normally a charge for each test/promotion. Sometimes, these fees are covered under the contract, and other times you are charged extra for each event.

Many schools insist students either participate in or observe a required number of competitions before testing to a particular rank. If the school doesn't organize or combine with other schools to offer local competitions, these extra costs can include registration for the events, transportation, lodging and food.

"Hidden Extras" That Can Add to the Cost of Lessons

The following items are sometimes found as part of a contract or as part of a school's "unwritten rules." They can run up the cost of lessons far beyond the amount of the tuition cost you initially agree to. Find out about these costs before you sign-up for lessons:

❏ Initiation Fees	❏ Membership Dues
❏ Registration Fees	❏ Promotion Fees
❏ Association Membership Fees	❏ Specialized Classes
❏ Private Lessons	❏ Down Payment
❏ Late Fees	❏ Finance Charges
❏ Reciprocal Benefits	❏ Required Equipment
❏ Transfer or Freeze Fees	❏ Required Uniforms/patches
❏ Attendance Limitations	❏ Competitions

Is There a Time Limit on the Contract?

A universal, standard martial arts contract does not exist. Each school develops its own or follows the traditional pay-by-month.

Contracts are binding agreements. Most states have a 72-hour or three-day cancellation policy for people who have second thoughts. Check your state laws for details regarding long-term contracts and your options.

Since contracts are often written for the benefit of a company or the person presenting it, they can be one-way. Ask questions. "A contract is not a contract until you sign it," a successful entrepreneur said.

Because the instructor states something is not a problem and not to worry about it, this does not absolve you from that part of the agreement. Cross out anything that raises concerns. If the instructor is unwilling to change the terms or clarify points, do not sign. Look for another school.

"If he's that inflexible," an experienced parent said when talking about making changes to contracts, "he'll be that way as a teacher. Walk away. Don't sign it."

Long-term contracts or agreements are not really practical for children. Lives are constantly changing. Families might have to move; children might decide they do not want to continue. Find out what your rights and options are before signing the contract. Will you receive a refund if you have paid the entire fee in advance and your family has to move? Some states have laws requiring schools to refund unused fees or transfer the membership if a student moves more than "x" miles from the school.

If the school is part of a chain, is the contract transferable to a school in another city? Sometimes, schools are loosely tied within a chain. If the instructor mentions other schools he or she is affiliated with, it may not be a transfer situation but more of an instructor network. Be sure to clarify what the instructor means by "affiliated with."

Contracts are meant to apply to the general population. Each family is an individual case. A good contract or agreement reflects both the family's needs as well as the school's.

⌛ Black Belt Contracts

Black belt contracts promise students will receive a black belt. Beware of instructors who make unrealistic promises and guarantee a black belt for a certain amount of money or in a very short period of time. Contracts often do not clarify whether students will actually learn the skills. Children may be pushed through the ranks in order to satisfy the contract. In these cases, the instructor shows no concern for a child's growth in the martial arts and will continually suggest the child test regardless of whether he or she is ready. This way, the instructor can hurry the child through the school and claim another black belt. If the student drops out, the instructor does not feel he has lost anything, because the student has already paid for more lessons than he has attended.

Some of these black belt contracts might not include the cost of black belt promotion, but simply take children to what schools designate is a junior or temporary black belt level. One father noted that for his daughter to test for black belt under the black belt contract (for which he had already paid in advance), he was required to pay another high fee in advance and sign his daughter to an additional multi-year contract.

Noticing his prepaid contract did not include a time limitation, he took advantage of that fact. It was no problem for him when his daughter wanted to stop for six months. Under the contract, he could restart her at any time. And he did.

Most schools include a time limit on the black belt contract. The contract should state this and clearly define what happens when a person is unable to achieve black belt in that time limit. For instance, does the black belt contract have to be repurchased or does the family have to pay (and how much) for an extension?

Many states are outlawing long-term black belt contracts. Some states have already passed regulations stating a one year contract is the maximum a school can sell.

Many states have also passed laws which require martial arts schools to be licensed as Health Clubs. States with club bonding laws require clubs charging membership fees to pay the state an annual fee. When martial arts schools which are designated health clubs under this law, do not pay the fee, they are put out of business. When licensed clubs go out of business unexpectedly, members may be able to recoup some or all of their unused fees through a state fund. Your library may have information on this law in your state.

⧗ Freezing a Contract

Injuries aren't common, but they can happen. Some are temporary such as a sprain and some are more permanent such as a bad knee. Students will miss practice. If the contract doesn't include an injury clause describing options if a major injury occurs, talk with the instructor and write one in.

⧗ Multiple Locations

Instructors with more than one facility in an area will have differing policies about their use. Some will not allow students at one facility to attend classes at the other. Others, who have built two or more facilities in an area, often encourage students to go to lessons at any of the locations.

⧗ Beware the Bait and Switch

As in any sales situation, unethical sales tactics such as the bait and switch can be used. Schools attract students with one price and then immediately push an extended black belt contract. Be aware of this tactic wo you will not fall prey to a high pressure bait and switch sales pitch.

Is One School Really Superior to All of the Others?

Some schools suggest (very authoritatively) they teach the only one effective martial arts system and talk negatively about their competitors. If the study of their martial art is broached as the cure-all for all concerns, this is an exaggeration and the school should be avoided.

What Is the Price/Value Ratio?

When considering the price and the value of what your child is receiving, take into account that it takes money to maintain a good facility. Many of today's schools are run as a business. Because they are successful, students have access to more facilities.

Concerned instructors try to build or remodel in order to create better facilities and conditions for their students. They look at safe locations and adequate parking, provide better equipment from targets to exercise machines, and use assistant instructors to ensure more individual attention during class.

Consider your as well as your child's goals and needs when evaluating the different schools. Look carefully at the atmosphere of the school and attitude of the other members before deciding on the right fit.

Include your child in the decision making process, and he or she will take ownership of the decision and have more incentive to make the experience succeed.

Part 3

Enjoying Your Martial Arts Experience

10

What to Expect Once Lessons Begin

Knowing what to expect can increase your child's enjoyment of the martial arts. Once lessons are started, your child assumes the responsibilities expected of all students and follows the rules established by the school.

Students learn to bow and to properly address upper belts and instructors. They might do a few push-ups for not bowing according to the school's rules, for not calling upper belts "Sir" or "Ma'am," or for being late.

Students are expected to arrive on time so they can get the full benefit of the workout from the preparatory stretches to the review of skills and introduction of new skills. It is also less disruptive to the entire class.

Conduct is important both in and out of the school. Doing things to the best of their abilities and developing confidence in themselves can translate to doing their best in other activities as well.

Students must be willing to ask questions and seek help. Practicing on their own, even for a few minutes before or after class is important.

Children must have a positive attitude toward class. This is shown by their willingness to learn and to help others learn. Those who complain about having to do a technique are closing their minds and also their bodies to learning. Accepting corrections and immediately adjusting their techniques, or trying to, will improve their skills. Students who are supportive and recognize the strengths of others, even those of lower ranks, keep themselves open to new skills and insights which can sometimes come from the most unexpected quarters.

What Is the Purpose of Promotion Tests?

Instructors and students use promotions (tests) as milestones to mark growing skills and knowledge. Each time students achieve another rank and another belt, they receive public recognition of their progress and self-affirmation of their knowledge.

New and more difficult skills are introduced to students who achieve the next rank. This builds upon the base of knowledge they already have and continues to help them set goals.

Just because a promotion is scheduled, does not mean your child has to test. Not all children test at every promotion or are expected to test at each opportunity. It is far more important children are ready and have successful testing experiences.

Promotion formats vary from school to school. Usually students are grouped into belt levels so they test with other students at or near their rank.

Students demonstrate their forms individually and in groups. They partner off and demonstrate self-defense skills, step-sparring, offensive and defensive techniques. Some schools include sections on board breaking and free-sparring. Judges can ask students questions regarding basic terminology and philosophy. In addition, students can be judged on their attitude during testing. Most students pass this section with flying colors!

Promotions can provide effective teaching and learning opportunities when judges take the time to communicate and teach as well as evaluate what students know.

Each school sets its own promotion schedules. Some conduct promotions every month, but usually establish rules which state students cannot test every month and list the number of classes which students must attend before testing for the next rank. This is a safeguard to help provide adequate time for students to learn the skills. Other schools establish a promotion schedule of every three to four months for all students who are ready to test.

Instructors encourage students to ask questions about what they can do to improve. Once children have this information, they are expected to make the necessary adjustments and practice so they will be ready for promotions.

A month or so after a promotion, some schools hold skill reviews. For about a two-week window of time, instructors will look at how well students know their new skills. If they do well, the instructor will do something tangible such as putting a strip of colored tape at the end of the belt. These students are counted as eligible to participate in the next promotion as long as other conditions are met.

Some hold pretests which act as check points. For instance, one pretest can assess a student's abilities to do hand and foot techniques. Another pretest will cover step-sparring, forms, stances and terminology. Each child is evaluated and given a sheet which critiques their skills. Once the pretest is passed, the student is ready for the regular promotion.

"Pretests help some students realize they're not ready to test," an instructor said.

For there are times during your child's martial arts experience when he or she will not be ready to test for the next rank. This can be due to a number of reasons including the number of lessons attended, the difficulty of the skills, the effort put towards learning and practice, prolonged illness, or family vacations.

When your child is not testing, he or she can still attend promotions. Your child's presence and support means a lot to the other classmates. As a side benefit, by observing and listening carefully, children can learn from the testing situation and be better prepared for the next promotion.

What is the Purpose of Extracurricular Demonstrations?

Many schools give demonstrations at schools, in malls and as part of special community celebrations. Students learn to appreciate the skills of others, build self-confidence and a shared history with students of all ages as they unite in preparing for a demonstration.

Participants attend special workout sessions to practice and perfect their skills for upcoming demonstrations. A school may even have an established demonstration team whose members wear special uniforms or insignia and hold regular practice sessions.

"It was fun making little skits showing that taekwondo can be fun," a student said about the practice sessions she had participated in when she was seven- and eight-years old.

Many children like performing in demonstrations because they get to go in front of people. "It's fun to show people what you've learned," said a teenager who had studied for four years.

One young man, a veteran of many demonstrations, said, "Demonstrations are a chance to show the beauty of the art form and to get rid of the myth that martial arts are used just to beat up people."

Is Earning a Black Belt the End of Lessons?

Achieving a black belt is just a beginning, not an end to a student's study of the martial arts. The student has learned the basics and can now build on them, continuing to grow.

Classes designed specifically for black belts and advanced students keep them involved and excited. These classes demonstrate the enormous room for growth in all aspects of a martial art once a person reaches the black belt level.

Some students who achieve black belt find this a good time to study another martial art. With their first art as a basis, they start again, but from scratch. As the ancient story states, you cannot fill a cup which is already full. In order to learn a new martial art with its different philosophies and techniques, the mind must be willing to accept new information.

Once they achieve black belt in another art, students have a broader base of knowledge to use themselves or to share with others. They can combine methods and select the tactics which work best for them, for their life-style, gender, age, and body build.

How Does a Student Become an Instructor?

As student's martial arts skills grow, many schools encourage them to develop their leadership and teaching skills.

Informal teaching opportunities occur during class when students are asked by the instructor to observe other students and tell them what they do well and demonstrate what is needed to improve.

Formal teaching opportunities are provided for those students who are selected to become assistant instructors. "They must be good technicians and have a genuine interest in helping out students," an instructor said.

But if students are dressed up in assistant instructor uniforms and put in front of the class without instruction, these teaching opportunities are simply window dressing. Leadership potential increases dramatically when assistants are given guidance and told what is expected of them. When this is followed with constructive feedback on what they did or did not do in class and how they responded to students, much growth will occur.

Good instructors meet with assistants individually or in special assistant instructor sessions to outline expectations, discuss options for various class behaviors, answer questions and help them make the most of their experiences.

Very organized and successful schools have a master instructor who teaches all instructors how to teach according to the school's and master instructor's overall philosophy. Then the master instructor assigns instructors to teach the classes and ages which interest them most and at which they will be most successful. Instructors are encouraged by the master instructor to research areas that interest them and share their findings with the other instructors.

"The master instructor provides consistency so everyone has access to the same information and is trained the same," said an instructor who researched and specialized in attention deficit students for the school.

11

How to Handle Boredom

At some point during their study, children might decide they want to quit. This, of course, brings up the "quit/discipline" paradox. Students want to quit. Yet, martial arts teaches discipline, and discipline means sticking with something. Guidance and input from parents can help children work through their difficult times.

If your child says he or she wants to quit completely, you could make them go to class. However, this is probably the worst thing you can do.

Before a power struggle begins, observe your child during classes. Once children arrive, meet their friends and start class, they often have a wonderful time. Knowing this in advance can give you a base from which to talk with your child to help clarify feelings and identify the real reasons behind the decision.

Children, like all of us, can come up with many reasons for quitting. You can gauge whether it's a one-time, "I want to stay home from class tonight," because they are overtired or sick, or whether it is something that creative approaches can help. Defining the cause of boredom is often the first step to conquering it. Below are some of the more common reasons children say they want to quit.

☹ Lack of Goals

Children become discouraged at times because they don't realize how far they have advanced and how much they now know. When children question their progress, they can review their short-term goals and see for themselves how much they have accomplished. They begin to realize goal setting is ongoing. Once they have succeeded at something they might have thought was impossible, they can become excited and set more goals. Helping your child set short-term goals which build toward completion of long-term goals is a key building block for a successful way of life.

When your child feels down, point out how much he or she has learned since the first week of class. These skills are becoming part of who your child is as a person.

☹ Slow Advancement

Children may decide to quit because they feel badly that they have not advanced to the next rank with other students who started with them. Possibly they were not ready to test at the same time as the others, or they attempted the test and failed. You can help your child understand that studying the martial arts is an individual journey. Everyone works at their own speed to improve their own skills, not to keep up with or pass others in the class.

☹ Inconsistent Parental Support

Parents greatly influence their children and their views toward life. If you complain about the instructor, the school, and the people there, this affects how your child approaches classes.

If parents and family members treat the study of the martial arts as a fill-in summertime activity, children will see it as such and their efforts will often be minimal. Martial arts viewed as a year-round activity becomes an accepted part of their lives.

☹ Excessive Pressure to Succeed

Some children are under too much pressure to succeed. This pressure can be self-induced or come from their instructor or parents. What you might view as a helpful suggestion, can be seen in your child's eyes as nagging, or as a sign he or she is not good enough. While meant to be helpful, the suggestions can increase the pressure to succeed.

☹ Excessive Criticism

Children can decide to quit if they receive too much criticism and negative feedback from the instructor. Children become tense and depressed if they think their instructor does not like them or does not believe they are any good. If lessons are not fun, there is no reason to go.

☹ Lack of Constructive Feedback

At the same time, children will question an instructor's motivation if the promotions are not as difficult or as thorough as the children thought the tests would be, or if they feel they are being pushed through the ranks.

"I thought the test was going to be hard, but it wasn't," a taekwondo student reported. "I felt I didn't do my best and didn't deserve to be promoted to the next level, yet they skipped me over a level."

☹ Repetition

Students can become bored with the repetitive nature of building a skill. It helps to recognize boredom as a natural interim or plateau which sometimes occurs before their next growth spurt. Keeping children focused on their goals might help them through plateaus. For others, taking a break from studying helps.

One student who often quit when she became bored, used these times to her advantage. "I tried something else for a time, but I always came back," she said. "When I came back, I was refreshed and ready to work a lot harder."

☹ Overcommitment

Sometimes children have too many commitments and priorities. In our quest to be perfect parents, to enable our children to experience a wide variety of activities so they can discover where their interests lie, we can over schedule. This is not healthy. Children should be encouraged to make their own decisions about which activities they want to commit their time and energy to. This way, they have time to devote themselves to success in their chosen areas, concentrate on school, and play with their friends.

☹ Burnout

If children focus entirely on martial arts, they can experience burnout and need a break. Sometimes a family vacation is enough; sometimes they need a longer time away from practice.

☹ Fear of Injury or Sparring

Some children quit because they are afraid of getting hurt during free-sparring, especially if they are in a school which fails to enforce safety rules.

Injuries incurred while playing other sports such as soccer, football, volleyball, basketball, track and tennis can also stop children from taking martial arts classes.

☹ Lack of Money

Children can quit because of lack of money. To combat this problem, some instructors have applied for grants which are available to help families afford lessons during difficult times. Other schools have scholarships funded by school events and fund-raisers.

☹ Aversion to Long-Term Commitment

As children progress in the martial arts, they begin to realize that learning a martial art takes commitment and dedication. A few might not be willing to give this.

There are times when it's best to accept your child's decision. "If a child doesn't want to come anymore to lessons," an instructor said, "I bring the child and the parent into my office and ask 'Why not? It's not going to hurt my feelings. I just want to know.' Sometimes, it's because a child misses play time with friends. That's okay. They can return later when they're more ready."

Is the Boredom Related to the School or Martial Arts in General?

Sometimes it is not general boredom which children feel, but a dissatisfaction with the instructor and the school. If the instructor does not have an overall plan, the school can flounder with no educational philosophy to guide it. An instructor who no longer puts forth the effort to plan may have lost his or her focus and enthusiasm—often without realizing it.

Instructors who set goals for their schools' futures keep the martial arts alive and exciting for themselves as well as their students. Enthusiastic instructors read books on teaching the martial arts and spend time thinking about and creating different, exciting ways to teach.

They teach skills by using activities which appeal to children. For instance, an aikido instructor tells teenagers and adults to walk across the floor on their knees to work on focusing, flexibility, and fluidity. To teach the same skill to young children, he has them walk on their knees across the mat while focusing on a balloon they are bouncing from hand to hand. Both groups are working on the same skill, but the children are taught through a fun game. Laughter frees children's minds and they learn more.

Boredom is less likely to occur during class if the instructor teaches many aspects of the martial arts, not just one. For instance, a class session emphasizing concentration can teach aspects of concentration through segments on self-defense, free-sparring, step sparring, balance, history, and terminology as well as basic and advanced offensive and defensive techniques.

Students who do not know what is expected of them at each level or where they are going, can become distracted and bored. Those who know what is expected of them at each belt ranking, have an easier time setting their own goals, recognizing how much they have learned since they began, and visualizing their own progress in the martial art. This encourages enthusiasm and direction for their personal study.

An instructor who compliments students in private after class, who offers a word of encouragement, who explains that perseverance can fill in when natural athletic ability falls short, and who develops class plans can contribute to your child's continued enthusiasm for the martial arts.

How Can I Help My Child Combat Boredom?

The search to find a school is significant to children's success. Investigating to find the best possible fit will eliminate some of the main reasons children quit. Prevention often works better than intervention.

The following are a few thoughts on what you and others can do to help your child enjoy classes.

☆ Is Your Child's Class the Right Age Group?

Being around others of their age group and making friends is part of an enjoyable martial arts experience. Feeling separated from the group can cause children to want to quit. Some children have successful experiences in schools without many children their age; others do not. Look for a school with a universal, accepting philosophy. Older students who include younger students in quick practice sessions before and after class; who talk, teach, and learn from them can help children feel a part of the group, regardless of their age.

☆ Do You Express an Interest in Your Child's Progress?

Expressing interest in your child's upcoming promotions and looking forward to going with them can enhance their excitement. Encouraging children to watch their friends' promotions, can help them feel part of the group.

☆ Are Others at the School Supportive of Your Child?

At times while they are growing up, children seem to respond better to anyone who is not their parent. The more people who are concerned about a child's well-being, the better for their growth into adulthood. When children are feeling less than positive, support from a trusted friend, close relative, or instructor can help them persevere.

One little girl cried when she didn't want to go to class. Her parents were going to have to take her home. The instructor simply reached out his hand to her and asked if she was going to be okay. "She ended up having a fantastic class," the instructor said.

☆ Do You Share the Instructor's Comments with Your Child?

Instructors often tell parents how their children are doing. "When parents ask me about their children," a karate instructor said, "I compliment them, but I add that they can be better. I say 'stick to it, train constructively and work hard.'"

Tell your child what the instructor said, emphasizing the positive points. Give your child something to be proud of, something to work on, and the rest will follow. Children, as well as adults, enjoy hearing about what they do well. Compliments are great motivators.

A woman commented she hadn't realized how much her son did around the house and yard until he broke his leg in football. When asked if she had told him this, she was shocked. "Of course not!"

Unfortunately, continually harping on the negative rather than emphasizing the positive will only make children nervous, angry and ultimately afraid to make a move. They can hide behind the phrase, "I never do anything right!" and, thus, not do anything.

Ongoing communication with children will help parents determine where children are in their martial arts studies. Everyone in the family can show their support with positive attitudes, discussions, and continued interest.

Real Life Profile

Kim, Barb, Michelle and Christine Talbot

A Family Goes All the Way: Starts Own school

If one of their daughters hadn't been beaten up by a neighbor boy, the Talbots would never have joined the martial arts and after eight years spent studying karate and taekwondo, made the major decision to start their own school.

"Martial arts, let alone owning our own school, just wasn't something we thought of when our children were little," Mr. Talbot said.

But after the incident: "We wanted the girls to handle themselves. Not so much to strike back, but to get out of situations," Mrs. Talbot said.

Mr. Talbot, who had taken some judo as a child, joined to help his daughters remember things from class to class. "I ended up getting sucked in."

Mrs. Talbot enrolled later after she settled into her new job and "also after seeing how the others did!"

The girls started lessons at eight and seven-years old. They believe their first major accomplishments were finally differentiating between right and left, forming a fist and doing their first kick and punch. Then their growth in the martial arts kicked into high gear.

"It's like learning how to walk," Michelle said. "Once you get the idea, you can take off. I was the type who could trip on air. After a few months, I noticed a huge change."

They had joined a school in which competitions were a major focus. At white belt rank, Mr. Talbot, Michelle and Christine found themselves competing regularly.

Finally, Mrs. Talbot competed. "I said I would do just one competition, just to see if I could do it," she said. "I continued competing for three years."

Competitions became special family events, mini vacations. They spent time driving around the country and, depending on the time of year, staying in hotels or at campsites.

Because of the age levels, the parents sometimes found themselves competing against each other in forms. But, Mrs. Talbot explained, since Mr. Talbot generally did so well, there was no real competition between them.

"I just wanted a reasonable placing," she said. "I was out there for the fun of it. But one day, a judge scored me higher than Kim. Made my day!"

Michelle and Christine first competed against each other when Christine was a brown belt. "The first time," Christine said, "I really wanted to beat her. I was jealous because she finessed everything. But I was sloppier because I put too much power in, and I lost. I was really upset."

Later that evening, they learned how to deal with their sibling rivalry and began to have fun competing against each other. "We always laughed it off after," Michelle said.

"I was usually happy I wasn't in last place," Christine said.

At the end of the tournament, they all looked forward to the parties and talking with the friends they'd made from around the country.

As a family in the martial arts, especially now that they have their own school with Mr. Talbot as the head instructor, they have enjoyed quite a few benefits, among them is the large amount of time they spend together.

"We all want to be active in our lives," Mrs. Talbot said. " This gives us a chance to do that and to be together."

Though once in awhile, the girls will groan at another night at the school, Michelle said, "It's fun. Martial arts is something we have in common, and there are very few things we have in common. We're all weird in our own ways, but we do taekwondo together."

Christine observed that many of their friends don't talk to their parents. "We have something we can talk about," she said.

"Like not going again!" Michelle laughed.

Mrs. Talbot observed that martial arts affirmed the positive values they instilled in their children. "It provided good role models, people who resist drugs and alcohol. Martial artists look down on drugs and alcohol."

"I teach the tenets of taekwondo and live the tenets, both in the school and at home," Mr. Talbot said.

They also expect their daughters to abide by the tenets. This proved difficult at times, especially when one daughter did not like a teacher in school and reacted badly in class. "Dad knew I was being a pain," she said. "If I didn't apologize, he was going to take me out of assisting. So I apologized."

Each member of the family has stories to tell in which they used nonviolent methods to protect themselves. Often, it is their self-confidence to stand up to others and not react fearfully that has gotten them out of situations—at work and on the street.

Once they decided to start their own school, things fell into place. They found a location above a warehouse which they could remodel into a school. Mr. Talbot asked and received special permission from his relatives in Japan to use the family crest as the school's logo.

The school emphasizes self-defense. Mr. Talbot teaches classes as well as special four session self-defense workshops. Many of the school's female students started with these workshops. "They develop confidence and realize they have the ability to defend themselves, and they want to learn more," he said. Businesses contract with him to teach these workshops to their employees.

Mr. Talbot also teaches special weapons classes including sai, nunchaka and bo. He points out that learning a weapon is part of martial arts, a more advanced way to defend oneself. "The weapon is an extension of the individual," he said.

Parents can watch their children in class through a large window. The Talbots make sure the parents understand the classes are for the children.

"How well or poorly a child does in class is not a reflection on the parent," said Mrs. Talbot who is also an instructor. "Parents shouldn't push children in the martial arts. We try to make classes fun. Martial arts is not learned instantly."

Mr. Talbot's attitude toward all students in the school is consistent. "Once I enter into the school and begin to instruct, they are not my wife and children. It took awhile for them to accept that," he said, then laughed. "I'm surprised at it working."

"We have people from the school over to our house," Michelle said, "and they're surprised to find out he's my dad."

Both parents see much positive growth in their daughters. "I'm proud of them. We constantly get compliments on their behavior outside of the home. I think that reflects directly on martial arts," Mr. Talbot said.

Michelle said the most important thing she learned was how to be confident and boisterous. Christine said she used to be boisterous and offend people and now has become more courteous and respectful of others.

For herself, Mrs. Talbot said, "It's a great way to blow off stress, especially after going to college during the day and dealing with too much work!"

Mr. Talbot credits the martial arts with helping him to focus more on life and family and providing positive ways to deal with stresses he finds at work.

Mr. Talbot sees his role as an instructor to provide information to students as well as motivation. "If the student is not willing to accept it, then it can reflect on me," he said. "I feel it's an accomplishment when one student thinks it's worth it."

12

Safety and Injury Protection

Parents' level of enjoyment and security regarding their child's study of the martial arts increases when safety worries decrease. Select a school that enforces safety rules including those pertaining to:

☝ Equipment

It should be clearly stated and posted in writing how old students have to be to use certain equipment or heavy bags as well as how to properly use mechanical equipment, bags, and targets.

Rules applying to correct target use should be repeated before each class use. For instance, the instructor or upper belts review with lower belts the correct procedures for holding targets based on the type of target and the skill to be practiced.

Some rules require students to work with partners who can control the heavy bag so the bag does not swing wildly around when kicked. In order to be effective, rules must be enforced and followed by everyone. When children watch a strong upper belt without a partner kicking the bag unmercifully, children sense a disrespect for the rules. This does not bode well for the school trying to teach an art based on discipline and respect. Punishments do not have to accompany every infraction. A simple reminder given immediately will suffice to enforce the rules.

☝ Sparring

To prevent injuries during free sparring practice, many schools establish contact rules. These will include where a person can punch or kick another based on the belt level of the lowest ranking partner; or the amount of contact whether it is none, light, or heavy. Contact rules are necessary to ensure safe practice.

Students should also be required to wear protective gear, even during non-contact sparring to ensure safety in the event of an accident. Safety gear can include head gear, chest protectors, forearm guards, shin guards, foam gloves, foam boots, a protective cup for boys and/or a mouth piece. The more contact that is allowed, the better protected students should be.

☝ Personal Hygiene

Wearing jewelry and chewing gum are banned during class. Jewelry can be easily broken or cause injuries to another or to oneself. Chewing gum can be swallowed or spit out.

Students are required to keep fingernails and toenails trimmed so they do not break the nails or scratch others.

☝ Illness

Sick children do not belong in class. Colds are easily spread through contact and shared gear or equipment. When children do not feel well, they often find it hard to concentrate. Their slower reactions could cause injury to themselves or others.

☝ Unsupervised Practice

When practicing outside of class or alone, children should warm-up first. They shouldn't try anything they have not been taught how to do in class.

Many schools offer open class times to people of all ranks and ages, while some will limit open time by either rank or age. If children are to take full advantage of open class times, they must be supervised and know what skills they want to work on. If possible, they can arrange with a higher ranking student or adult to work with them.

Open class times can turn into useful practice sessions, but since they are loosely run and space is limited, accidents may happen. Someone, either an instructor or a black belt, should be designated to supervise open workout times and ensure all students follow safety rules.

How Can the Instructor Increase Class Safety?

To prevent muscle injuries during class, each session should automatically start with conditioning exercises (warm-ups, stretching, balance, strength, and endurance) and end with a cool down period. Students in good condition can better perform the skills.

Instructors who are attuned to the emotional tone of the class can adjust their class plan at the last minute, based on what they observe. For instance, if members are sparring too aggressively, the instructor can alter the plan and stop the sparring altogether or institute something unusual to put students off-balance and demand they pay close attention. This could be something as simple as sparring with their favored hands behind their backs.

After a long weekend, many students at Monday night classes might not be mentally and physically focused on class activities. If they are not up to the performance level required for the lesson plan, the instructor must be willing and able to switch plans. This will prevent injuries which can be caused by carelessness.

For certain class activities, the instructor uses discretion and alters the usual random mix of partners and pairs students based on their size, age, sex, strength and ability.

What Types of Safety Equipment Are Used?

Sparring gear, to be of any use, must fit correctly and be in good condition. Torn gear should be replaced immediately.

Protection gear requirements vary from school to school and from martial art to martial art. Basic gear usually consists of a soft padded helmet, gloves, feet protectors, shin guards, rib or chest guard, mouth guard, elbow/forearm pads, and for males (and possibly females), a sports cup.

Does the School Require a Medical Permission Form?

It is always a good idea for parents of children involved in sports to sign a note giving permission for medical treatment if the parents aren't present. Academic schools commonly do this. The release form should include the name of your child's doctor, the medical phone number, and your signed permission for emergency medical treatment.

If your child has pre-existing medical problems, discuss them with the instructor. Most schools do not require physicals before allowing students to sign-up. It will be up to you to inform the instructor of potential problems that could affect your child's time in classes. The instructor can then be prepared for any emergencies.

Are First Aid Supplies and Training Provided?

Injuries do not happen often. However, when people get careless, overtired or have not been properly taught how to do a technique, injuries can occur.

Many schools have someone with first-aid training (usually an instructor or assistant) present during classes and an easily accessible first-aid kit. Ideally, all of the school's instructors would have first-aid training, but this is not always the case.

In well-run schools, major injuries are rare. Even common injuries such as bruises, muscle pulls, and sprains do not often occur. Studies have proven martial arts to have lower injury rates than common sports like gymnastics, football, basketball and bike riding. However, in schools which concentrate on contact fighting, there can be more frequent and severe injuries, including head and facial injuries.

The instructor can discuss the type of injuries and the number of injuries which have occurred in the school over the past year as well as describe the insurance which the school carries.

Is Proper Conditioning Taught?

Out of shape students become winded and have poor endurance for physical activities. Martial arts workouts provide a variety of conditioning activities and exercises which enhance flexibility, strength, stamina, speed, and aerobic capability. Through regular class attendance, students become fit and maintain healthy fitness levels.

Emphasizing basic conditioning decreases the likelihood of common injuries. Warm-ups and stretches prepare the muscles and body for the workout. Students in good physical condition have more endurance, strength, and flexibility.

However, proper exercising must be accompanied by proper nutrition. Children who eat healthy diets have the strength to perform to their maximum capabilities and have greater abilities to concentrate and focus their attention during workouts and sparring sessions.

What Activities May Be Harmful?

Physical therapists often recommend certain exercises and activities be done after a person has at least reached middle school years, because these exercises create too much pressure on joints and cartilage. Children should not do open hand push-ups, deep knee bends and strength activities such as straight leg sit-ups. (In fact, people of all ages should avoid these exercises.)

✖ Push-ups

Correctly done knuckle push-ups are better than open hand push-ups. "Open hand push-ups put an unusual amount of strain on the wrist joint and cause the joint to be hyperextended," said a chiropractor who studied the martial arts for several years. "A knuckle push-up, although somewhat difficult to do at times, aligns bones. It allows the bones of the hand and the wrist to be lined up with the bones of the forearm. This is certainly less stressful to the wrist. New students can be encouraged to let their knees touch the ground and do half-push ups."

✖ Bouncing Stretches

Bouncing during stretching exercises can be harmful to all students. Students should work on stretching their muscles, not bouncing from one count to the next. They must also remember stretching is not a contest. The goal is to improve their own stretch, not compete with their neighbor to see who can go the highest or stretch the farthest.

✖ Repetitive Exercises

Repetitive training exercises and activities should be symmetrical and performed using both right and left sides. This will enhance coordination on both sides of the body as well as symmetry and balance in muscle function and appearance.

✖ Excessive Jumping

Excessive jumping on hard floors puts unwanted stress on knee and ankle joints. Students must be taught how to land properly in order to minimize the stress.

✖ Forced Stretching

Children between the ages of eleven and fourteen are growing and their legs are disproportionately longer than their trunks. This makes it basically impossible for them to sit on the ground and touch their toes with their fingertips. They could before they entered this growth spurt, and they will do so afterwards. Their muscles are not tight. Stretching exercises might help keep them limber but will not enable them to touch their toes until after they have finished growing.

✖ Assisted Stretches

Stretching exercises involving assistance from a partner are not appropriate for children unless closely supervised by an adult. These include exercises in which one student applies pressure to another to help improve the student's stretch. For example, one student sits cross-legged on the ground while another student pushes forward on the person's shoulders. Another exercise for young children to avoid is performed by one student standing under another's leg and slowly lifting it higher. Also, mechanical stretching machines should be used only by older students.

✖ Weight Training

Weight training develops strength and involves lifting weights or wearing weights while exercising. Weight training can be detrimental to young children, but is often beneficial and fun for middle school students.

✖ Heavy Bag Striking

An organized heavy bag training routine should wait until children are ready. Size, strength, coordination and skill level are all factors that determine when a child's body can withstand heavy bag striking.

✖ Contact Sparring

Full-contact sparring can be held off until children are in their teens. For many schools, sparring is "recreational" and there is no full-contact practice, but only light or moderate contact practice. In these schools, children can start sparring at the same point in their study that all students begin sparring.

Schools that concentrate on sparring often want their competitors to gain or lose weight in order to have an advantage in the competitive ring. Telling children to "make weight" puts unnecessary pressure on them and can distort their views of what is healthy. Children's bodies must be allowed to grow and develop naturally. Weight enhancing drugs and anabolic steroids should be avoided as should diuretics and crash or fad diets. Following good nutritional guidelines in conjunction with physical activities should be the only weight maintainence program advocated for healthy children.

✖ Board Breaking

Board breaking techniques should be adjusted to fit children's sizes. Young children's fists are too small to break boards. The most appropriate punch for a small fist is a hammer punch, in which the soft side of the hand absorbs the force. Punches in which the knuckles and wrist absorb force should not be practiced until a child is physically mature. Children have more kicks to choose from since their feet and heels are stronger than their fists. A side kick is a good one to use to break boards.

Some schools will base the size of the board to be broken on children's weights. For instance, children under 60 pounds will break a 1" thick board that is 6" by 12". Children weighing between 60 and 80 pounds will break 8" boards and those above 100 pounds will break 10 1/2" boards. Other schools provide the same size for all students.

✖ Early or Contact Weapons Training

Weapons classes often require instructor approval and are usually open to students who are at least at the intermediate level.

"Some schools start students too soon on weapons. The students don't adequately learn the basics before concentrating too much on weapons," an instructor said.

Weapons training always requires coordination and focus, both of which develop at varying times in children. Younger students can study weapon techniques which are taught in weapon forms and involve no contact with other students. Students of all ages often begin weapons training with special practice weapons such as foam rubber covered nunchakus so when they hit themselves while practicing, they won't bruise themselves as they would with the actual weapon.

Weapons training taught as a contact class should be limited to older students. For example, a school which teaches escrima (Philippine fighting sticks) as a contact class requires students to be seventeen years old and to wear hockey gloves and head gear.

Maintaining Facility and Equipment

An instructor implementing standards for maintenance and cleanliness of the facility and its equipment shows concern for the health of everyone in the school. A well-maintained, clean facility decreases and helps prevent exposure to unnecessary risks as well as germs.

Equipment kept in good repair and working order helps prevent injuries. Students are less likely to injure or cut themselves on exercise equipment which is not broken. If the school supplies sparring equipment for all students to share, the equipment should be cleaned thoroughly between each use. This can help prevent the spread of colds and in the case of head gear—lice.

Real Life Profile

Justin Margotto

Ranked # 1 in the Nation for 3 Years

"At first, competition was no big deal," Justin Margotto said. "At six years old, I just wanted to win a trophy."

Ten years later, after being acclaimed #1 in the nation in forms for three of those years, he says, "It's an honor to win. I learned to appreciate it more."

Justin was in kindergarten when his parents signed him up for martial arts classes.

"I was freaked out at the first class," he said. "I didn't want to do karate. I was afraid of ninjas. But once I put on the uniform, it was cool."

According to Gary, Justin's father, "Once he put on the uniform, he was gone: hook, line and sinker."

Winning requires focus and commitment, a dedication to reaching a goal. Justin, who was diagnosed with ADD (Attention Deficit Disorder) at an early age, found karate gave him more than trophies and titles. "The biggest things karate has done has helped me with my concentration and discipline," he said.

Karate also taught him how to treat other people. "I was horrible at it," he said. "Once I started karate, I learned to value friends and to make friends. I used to be so shy and not talk to anybody. Now I can talk to anybody I want." He enjoys the attention of young students from other studios who ask for his autograph and take his picture. "Everybody treats you nicely."

He competes in forms and weapons (bo) on the state, regional and national levels. In each of the three years he ranked first in the nation, Justin competed in 11 national tournaments outside of his home state of Wisconsin. For four of those years, Justin won a place on a national team, and for two of those years, the team paid his expenses.

Because of the time and money required to compete successfully at this level, his parents have also made a strong commitment. But it was worth it. Gary states that the most important aspect of the competitions was to see Justin win and try his best. "His first big first place was a large accomplishment," Gary said.

To prepare for national competitions, Justin takes private lessons once or twice a week, practicing more for his weapons routine than for his form routine. "Weapons takes longer to learn because there's more things to learn and more parts to pay attention to," Justin said. "There's a standard form in our studio for bo. I can't make up a form." Justin competes with a bo, but also practices the nunchaku, tonfa and sai.

Justin advocates patience for those children who want to compete on the national level. "You have to build up your strength to compete and build up time to get first place. You need the right mental and physical attitudes for karate."

He doesn't train all-out when it's close to the competition date, because he doesn't want to injure himself. He depends on his adrenaline kicking in during the competition to give him the winning edge. "It's impossible for me to do a routine in practice the same way I do it in a tournament," he said. "In practice, there's not as many people running around and there's less excitement and adrenaline."

He said he becomes nervous before each competition. "But," his father said, "if Justin is not nervous, then we have a problem."

Justin has developed his own method to prepare for each competition. "Right before I compete, I like to be by myself, concentrate and clear my mind, and listen to upbeat music to get my adrenaline going," he said.

He's learned not to worry or judge how well the other people are doing. "It's not up to me, but to the judges," he said.

He also looks practically at the situation. "If they're good, fine. If they're bad, even better."

Justin has a good memory and the ability to adapt his form to any type of music. "The form I'm using now took two days to create, and I did it about six months ago," he said.

Justin counts as a major benefit of competition the number of friends he's made from across the nation. But he doesn't allow friendships to interfere with his competitive edge. "We're friends before the tournament and after it," Justin said. "At the competition, we're not friends. I just want to win."

The main drawback with ranking first in the nation, Justin discovered, is that people know what he's capable of. They know they have to beat him in order to win.

Recently, Justin became an instructor for the gold belt class in his studio. Teaching has opened a whole new vista of opportunities for Justin. "I like teaching," he said. "It's part of what I do." Disciplining students is something he faces weekly. "If they're doing something I don't want them to do, I give warnings. Parents have to expect their children to work on learning and concentration," he said.

Justin's students benefit from his experiences of growing up in the martial arts. "I was a brat when I started," Justin said. "I've matured quite a bit. I don't get upset at things the way I used to. I tell my students how to control themselves, give them something else to do and have fun. Concentrating for a half-hour is tough for any kids who are five and six-years old. But their concentration gets better as they progress."

So far, Justin has won 215 trophies at national, regional and state tournaments. He ranked first in the nation in forms and weapons in 1992, and first in forms in 1993 and 1995. The school Justin belongs to named him Student of the Year in 1991, 1992, and 1996. For almost five years, Wisconsin Public Television's opening to *Get Real*, a series about outstanding youth, featured Justin performing a flying side kick.

13

Competitions

Students who want to compete can choose among local, regional and national competitions. Local competitions may be sponsored by a school or chain of schools. Regional competitions may cover several states. National competitions are held throughout the United States.

Competitions can be *closed*, which means that only students of one martial arts style or one school or a selected group of schools may enter. Competitors of all schools and styles can participate in *open* tournaments.

Until children gain experience in both types of competitions, they can be intimidated by the unfamiliar. A father described how his young son who often took first place at traditional taekwondo competitions was intimidated at an open tournament by "the loud music from the musical forms, the flashy uniforms, the abundant screaming. Fortunately, my son was later able to assess the situation and call upon his past tournament successes so he kept motivated and continued to compete at both traditional and American (open) style tournaments."

In competition, students are grouped according to their ages and rankings. They can choose to compete in forms, musical forms, free-sparring, weapons, board breaking (found in traditional taekwondo tournaments), showmanship (choreographed self-defense skits), team events, and other events as decided by the people or organizations running the tournament.

An instructor who also serves as president of a tournament circuit notes tournaments build confidence in children regardless of their preferred competition event. "Eventually children are drawn to a certain type of competition," he said. "Some only like forms and not sparring or weapons. Others like them all."

What Sort of Rules Are Used in Competition?

For each tournament, a basic set of rules are enforced. Referees and judges, especially at the national level, are formally trained. Organizers of local and regional tournaments will meet with the judges to review ground rules before the tournament starts.

Judges must base their decisions on common elements of the martial arts such as power, concentration, speed, and balance and judge how well the techniques are performed.

It can be hard for a judge from a soft style kung fu background to judge a hard style karate student. It can also prove difficult to judge students from different schools, even if they are studying the same martial art. While doing the same form, students may vary their movements slightly, because they are following the format taught by their individual schools.

"I believe judges really try to do their best to be unbiased, score forms fairly, and call free-sparring points accurately," a judge said. "However, difficulties occur because judges come from a variety of martial arts backgrounds and were taught by instructors with different philosophies. What one judge considers a point may be too far away from the target for another judge. What one judge may consider appropriate contact, another may consider excessive."

In open tournaments, time limits for forms, musical forms, and weapons routines are normally three minutes. The countdown begins as soon as the judges call the competitor's name. The three minutes includes the competitor's introduction, routine and conclusion. Following these guidelines, many forms competitors learn a two minute form. They are not penalized as long as their complete routine is under three minutes.

Students demonstrate forms existing in their martial art or a forms routine which they or their instructor create. Many martial artists perform their routines to music.

Competitive sparring is different from self-defense fighting. It's really point sparring. Children and lower belts in many open tournaments have a total of two minutes of continuous fighting. If the judges call a point, the time clock stops until they are lined up and ready to fight again. The winner is the first person who reaches five points or who is ahead at the end of two minutes.

Under different rules, black belt sparring in taekwondo national tournaments consists of three rounds which are three-minutes each, with a one-minute rest period between rounds. The competition is not stopped for points, which are announced at the end of each round or at the end of the match.

Weapons competition consists of competitors performing forms with a variety of weapons, often to music. Students are judged on how dynamic their presentations are and how focused they appear to be. Judges look for correct and realistic use of weapons as well as clean and crisp techniques.

How Are Competitions Ranked?

Students can compete for regional and national rankings. They earn points toward national rankings when they compete in regional and national competitions certified by a ranking body. For instance, AAA, AA and A nationals and BBB tournaments will earn national ranking points. Winners at competitions with higher rankings (AAA) will earn proportionately more points than those of lower ranked competitions. Competitions are ranked based on their level of competitiveness and the number of competitors they attract. National points count toward regional rankings, but regional points (BB and B tournaments) do not count toward national rankings.

Students have to compete often to get their name noticed and to earn points toward national ranking. Luck plays a factor unless students are already ranked in the top five. The others select a number which determines the order in which they will compete. The rule of thumb is that it is better to compete near the end or at the end of the group.

Why Do Students Compete?

Students compete for a variety of reasons. Some compete for the experience. Some want to know how their skills match up against others. Some compete to build their confidence. Others compete because their schools require them to have this experience before they can test for black belt. Others compete because their schools promote competitions and teach their students how to compete.

"I feel competition can empower people and build confidence and self-image if they are not forced to compete," said an instructor whose studio promotes competition.

A teenager who began competing at age six, explained that, at first, it was "no big deal." He just wanted a trophy. As he progressed, his views matured. "You appreciate it more," he said. "It's an honor to win."

Another instructor with almost thirty years of teaching said, "A martial arts tournament is a contest of skill and power. Although the competitive spirit of all participants is important, students should also enjoy the event and take advantage of it for making new acquaintances, exchanging techniques, and spreading the attributes of the art to the spectators."

Not all children will compete or are expected to participate in competitions. Many schools do not encourage or promote competitions. In these schools, it is up to the children and their parents whether they choose to participate in competitions.

How Can My Child Prepare for Competition?

Instructors have differing philosophies on competitions and how to prepare for them.

Some hold competition training classes in which students take roles as judges or as competitors. As judges, they gain an understanding of what to look for from competitors. As competitors, they practice introducing themselves to the judges and performing their competitive routine.

Some instructors just answer a few questions about competitions after class if the student raises the subject. Other instructors believe parents should sign-up their children in a competition and let them learn by experience.

Rather than go blindly into the competitive arena, families can first observe a tournament in their area or take a mini-vacation and observe a tournament further away. Doing this before actually entering a competition can clear up many misconceptions and create much excitement. It can also help avoid bad experiences which can take the joy out of studying the martial arts.

A young boy, extremely excited about an upcoming competition, invited his father who lived 300 miles away to watch. The boy had never attended a competition before, and his instructor hadn't told him what to expect.

The boy assumed free-sparring involved several rounds and opponents, and since he trained in a school which enforced free-sparring rules, he didn't know that attitude wasn't taught at all schools. He lost and was disappointed he couldn't sign-up for any other event that day. "It turned my son off," the father said. "He didn't want to continue to be a part of the martial arts."

The son, who turned his interest to flying, quit studying the martial arts. He had liked his teacher and the school's attitude. He had earned the money and paid for the classes himself. But he felt betrayed because he wasn't properly prepared for competitions.

Proper preparation so children know what to expect can turn tournaments into motivating and learning experiences.

"Fighting is rougher at tournaments," one competitor said. "You have to fight people you haven't seen before, and you don't know how they fight. But in tournaments you learn more."

It helps if the children's instructors are present and can offer support. "You've got to encourage your students," an instructor said. "Everyone wants the big prize. But if you give 100 percent, are you a failure? No. If someone beats you, you haven't failed. The important part is to be able to say, 'I tried my best.'"

Students win even if they lose by how they evaluate what they did and work to improve their skills for the next competition. Their attitude remains positive, and they don't blame everyone else for their defeat.

How Does a Typical Competition Proceed?

Competitions are held in large areas such as gymnasiums or hotel meeting rooms which can be opened into an arena with smaller rooms used as extra competition rings.

The main competition arena is divided into square rings with narrow walking spaces in-between. Judges will sit on one side of the ring. Competitors line up on the other. They select numbers which determine their order of competition.

Only competitors, judges, and instructors are allowed on the floor. Parents, siblings, and non-competing supporters sit on the sides or in bleachers.

Competitors should prepare their bodies ahead of time to handle the extra physical demands competitions spark. The time to master the routine is before competition day.

At the tournament, prior to competing, competitors warm-up and walk through their routine. Some imagine presenting themselves to the judges and doing their routines. Others go off by themselves to concentrate and psyche themselves for the event. Others like to warm-up in a group.

Schools set protocol they expect their students to follow in order to introduce themselves and their events to the judges. Usually, students bow before entering the ring, then bow before the judges. They introduce themselves and the school they represent, give the name of their form and ask whether they can begin. Since the presentation varies from school to school, judges look most closely at the level of confidence and respect shown by competitors.

Being late, disorganized, or displaying a bad attitude can affect how the judges look at a routine. As competitors gain experience on the circuit, the judges will get to know them. "They can tell if I'm not competing at my highest level," a young competitor said.

Sometimes judges make bad decisions. Sometimes people haven't been grounded in the philosophy of the martial arts, and do unethical things in order to win a trophy. In cases of parental disagreement with a decision or wrong doing, parents can talk with their child's instructor and let the instructor discuss the decision with the judges.

In one case, a yellow belt's jaw was injured by her opponent. The instructor talked with the paramedics and then the arbitrator. Since there was supposed to be no contact at yellow belt level, the competitor was awarded first place. Later, it was discovered her opponent was an advanced belt kick boxer (even though only a yellow belt in this martial art) and was using this competition to prepare for an upcoming kick boxing competition. The instructor pointed out to her that as a yellow belt she had blocked everything except that one kick. She was hooked, worked on free-sparring techniques with her instructor, and competed whenever she could.

Many instructors who are closely involved in competitions suggest parents leave the coaching to the instructors. Children face the judges and their contemporaries on their own. At this time, a supportive word and handshake from the coach can mean more than suggestions from parents.

"You have to be patient," a competitor's parent said. "You find yourself telling other parents not to get mad at their children for what they do. If my child makes a mistake, it's a part of life. I'll go to the next tournament and tell him 'to do your best.'"

To increase your child's chances of having an enjoyable and successful competition experience, encourage him or her to compete in an area in which the school specializes.

What Does It Take to Win at the National Level?

Years of hard work and dedication on the part of the competitor as well as instructors and parents are required to participate successfully on the national tournament.

"Effort has to go with perseverance," an instructor said. "If they tell me they want to be a champ, they have to do this, this, and this. If the words out of their mouths don't match their training, they're not going to make it."

National tournaments attract some of the most accomplished martial artists. To compete at this level, competitors have to intensify their practice sessions and fine-tune their techniques and stances.

"We emphasize stances, power, speed, and kihaps in our competition training," a karate instructor said.

"I work to make my form more realistic, with no hesitation," a national competitor said. "I practice my form facing different directions since I've no idea how the ring will look."

Competitor's attitudes must be focused on improving their routines. If they are willing to work hard and listen to the critiques of their instructor or other trusted individuals, their chances of placing and earning points toward national ranking can improve.

National competitors often practice longer and take more lessons than other students. One or two private lessons a week, even a half-hour long, can help them perfect their routines and become physically and mentally ready to compete.

To build endurance and aerobic capability, competitors can run or work on equipment such as an exercise bike or trampoline jogger. A series of drills which develop their breathing, concentration, and techniques should become cornerstones of their practice sessions.

However, more is required of a competitor than a good attitude, extra lessons, and practice time. Parents are major factors in children's successes. National competitions are held on weekends throughout most of the year. The more tournaments children successfully compete at, the more points they will earn toward national ranking.

Many weekends during the school year are spent traveling around the country. A strong commitment to competing nationally involves the cooperation of the children's academic schools and teachers as well as the children and their parents. Many Fridays will be missed, and children will have work to make up.

Parents will also miss many Fridays at work. "It's a commitment," a parent said. "I'd miss at least one day of work when there was a tournament. It could be as often as twice a month."

It is expensive to travel to national tournaments. Some may be within driving distance, but most will require flying. In addition to entry costs and transportation, parents will have to consider food and hotel costs.

Once children are well-known and successful on the national circuit, they may be picked up and sponsored by a national team who will help pay expenses.

14

Martial Arts for the Whole Family

A new world usually opens for families who take martial arts together. Parents and children have an entire form of communication and experiences that belong just to them.

"It's fun. Something we all do together, practice at home and talk about," said a high school student about his family's experience in the martial arts.

Stronger family relationships can build from this common ground. A father joined the martial arts a year after every other member in his family had enrolled. He was able to ask his children, including his eight-year old, for help in learning his forms and for critiques on his techniques. This improved the children's self-esteem and confidence. They could then ask him for practical self-defense techniques and practice on him techniques which would work against large people.

Another father who competes on the regional and national circuits depends on his family to critique his form. "They're pretty hard on me," he said. "But their insight has helped me improve."

A brother and sister in high school spent time outside of class developing a team routine which they used in competition and for demonstrations. When their mother enrolled in the martial arts, she was able to offer constructive advice and even enter a few events of her own when she drove them to competitions.

What Are the Benefits of Martial Arts?

People of all ages benefit intellectually and physically when they study the martial arts. Adults discover they are not expected to know everything just because they are older. They can learn a new skill step by step just like everyone else and work at their own pace.

The martial arts can help keep minds sharp and bodies moving. One husband told his wife the morning after her first class that it was the first time in years that he had not seen her hobbling when she first got up.

Students develop better eye/hand coordination. With practice, they can gauge how far they are from a target. They become comfortable using their hands or feet and competent with both sides of their body, regardless of whether they are right- or left-handed. Class activities, which require them to look first for an open target before reacting, enable them to improve reaction times.

Many reactions become automatic. Students learn self-defense techniques and attitudes and sharpen their awareness of their surroundings. "You have to be aware of everything around you," a teenage girl said. "I want to know the shadow next to me is my own."

Students learn words in another language, study history and culture, and gain a broader view of the world.

They develop a strategy of winning in which they can win at least two ways: through the actual event and by their attitude.

People can begin taking lessons at any age and be successful. Some are better at the physical aspects, others are better at the intellectual skills, while some excel at both. All students can work to the best of their abilities and succeed, getting out of their martial arts studies what they put into them.

Part 4

Evaluation Forms

School Evaluation Form

Complete one form for each school you are considering. You may make unlimited copies of this questionnaire for your personal use. Some questions may be answered while you are making telephone inquiries and many more may be answered during your visit to the school and trial lesson. While you will probably not be able to answer every question, answering as many questions as possible for each school will help you make an educated decision when the time comes.

Once you have completed the forms, you can perform a side-by-side, point-by-point comparison to help you objectively compare the schools. This questionnaire is not meant to make a decision for you, so there are no correct answers or scoring systems provided. Instead, it is intended to serve as a place for you to summarize your findings as you prepare to make an informed decision with your child.

Important Note: If you have borrowed this book from a public library, **please photocopy these pages** so the next person may benefit from them.

Part 1. General Information:

School Name _____

Address _____

Phone _____   Instructor's Name _____

Style(s) Taught _____

Number of years the school has existed at this location _____ years

Travel time to the school _____ minutes

Notes _____

_____

_____

Part 2. Exterior Evaluation:

1. Adequate parking (lot and/or street) ❑ Yes ❑ No

2. Adequate lighting in parking area ❑ Yes ❑ No

3. Adequate lighting at entrance to building ❑ Yes ❑ No

4. Condition of the parking lot ❑ Good ❑ Fair ❑ Poor

5. Safety of neighborhood after dark ❑ Good ❑ Fair ❑ Poor

Notes _____

_____

_____

Part 3. Instructor/Owner

1. Rank: _____ degree black belt

2. Number of years martial arts experience _____

3. Number of years teaching _____

4. Education _____

5. Affiliation/Certification _____

6. Number of instructors _____

7. Number of assistants _____

8. Qualifications of assistant instructors _____

9. Qualifications of instructors _____

10. Basic philosophy of the school _____

_____

_____

_____

11. Main focus of the school is   ❑ self-defense/self-protection

                                     ❑ forms/traditional skills

                                     ❑ sparring/competition

                                     ❑ all of above

                                     ❑ other _____

12. Does the instructor teach weapons? ❑ Yes   ❑ No

     If yes, what kinds? _____

     If yes, at what rank/age does weapons practice begin? _____

Notes _____

_____

_____

_____

Part 4. Class Schedule:

1. Number classes offered per week? _____

2. Days and times of classes:

   Day _____   Time _____

   Day _____   Time _____

   Day _____   Time _____

   Day _____   Time _____

3. Classes are: ❏   unlimited attendance

   ❏   limited to _____ classes/week

   ❏   limited attendance until _____ belt

4. Classes are for: ❏ children ages _____   ❏ mixed age group

5. Who teaches class?   ❏ head instructor   ❏ assistant instructor

6. There are _____ instructors/assistants for a class of _____ children.
   ___(number)___   ___(number)___

7. Does the instructor use a written class plan for each class?

   ❏ Yes   ❏ No   ❏ Don't Know

8. Is there a written goal or mission statement for the school?

   ❏ Yes   ❏ No   ❏ Don't Know

9. How many classes are required to promote to each belt rank? _____

10. Are written requirements for each rank available?   ❏ Yes   ❏ No

11. School's extracurricular activities include:

    ❏ demonstrations   ❏ competitions   ❏ parties

    ❏ private lessons   ❏ special classes   ❏ seminars/workshops

    ❏ other _____

Notes _____

_____

_____

Part 5. Safety Record:

1. What types of injuries have occurred? _____

2. What does the school's insurance cover? _____

3. Does it cover medical costs?   ❏   Yes   ❏   No

4. Does it cover liability?   ❏   Yes   ❏   No

5. Does it cover injuries at tournaments? ❏   Yes   ❏   No

6. Does it cover injuries at other events? ❏   Yes   ❏   No

Part 6. Costs

1. **Tuition Cost** $_____

2. Length of program _____

3. Tuition includes:

      ❑ Group lessons (_____ per week)

      ❑ Private lessons (_____ per week)

      ❑ Test fees

      ❑ Uniform

      ❑ Other _____

4. Other fees that may be incurred: (enter cost, if any, per term of contract)

      ❑ Promotion Fees $_____

      ❑ Special Classes Fees $_____

      ❑ Registration $_____

      ❑ Association Membership $_____

      ❑ Late Fees $_____

      ❑ Taxes $_____

      ❑ Uniform/patches $_____

      ❑ Other $_____

      Total Additional Fees $_____

          + Tuition Cost $ _____ = **Total Fees** $_____

To accurately compare schools, divide the amount on the Total Fees line by the number of months in the contract. Then, compare the total monthly cost for each school.

5. Is any required equipment, such as a uniform, included in the cost of the initial payment?   ❑ Yes   ❑ No

    If yes, what? _____

6. Is any equipment required to be purchased?   ❑ Yes   ❑ No

    If yes:

        Item _____   Cost $_____

        Item _____   Cost $_____

        Item _____   Cost $_____

7. Can used equipment be purchased?   ❑ Yes   ❑ No

8. Necessary equipment can be purchased:

    ❑ at the school

    ❑ through a mail order catalog

    ❑ at a local sports or consignment goods store

9. Can equipment be shared by students?   ❑ Yes   ❑ No

10. Will additional equipment be required as the child advances?

    ❑ Yes   ❑ No

    If yes:

        Item _____ Cost $_____ Needed when? _____

        Item _____ Cost $_____ Needed when? _____

        Item _____ Cost $_____ Needed when? _____

11. Are memberships transferable to other people?   ❑ Yes   ❑ No

   If yes, how? _____

12. Are members allowed to attend classes in other branches at no cost?

   ❑ Yes ❑ No   If yes, where? _____

13. Can membership be frozen and restarted later for any reason?

   ❑ Yes ❑ No   If yes, are there limitations? _____

14. Can membership be frozen if a child becomes injured?

   ❑ Yes ❑ No   If yes, are there limitations? _____

15. If you move out of town, can you obtain a refund of the unused portion of the contract?   ❑ Yes ❑ No

16. How long do you have to cancel the contract and obtain a full refund?

   _____ days from the date of signing

Part 7. Facility:

1. Is the classroom an adequate size?   ❑ Yes ❑ No

2. Is the waiting area an adequate size?   ❑ Yes ❑ No

3. Is there a separate area to practice before class?   ❑ Yes ❑ No

4. Are the locker room locations appropriate?   ❑ Yes ❑ No

5. What equipment is included in the membership fee?

_____

6. Is the classroom clean and safely furnished?   ❑ Yes ❑ No

7. Is equipment well maintained?   ❑ Yes ❑ No

8. Are the bathrooms/lockers clean?   ❑ Yes ❑ No

9. Is a water fountain available?   ❑ Yes ❑ No

Part 8. Trial Class Evaluation

This section should evaluate a trial lesson in the class your child will normally participate in after signing-up.

1. Number of students in class: _____

2. Colors of children's belts: _____

3. Age range of students in class: _____

4. Does class begin and end on time?   ❑ Yes   ❑ No

5. Number of instructors and assistants present: _____

6. Atmosphere of class: (ex. enthusiastic, positive attitude, professional, disciplined learning environment, rigid, monotonous, out of control)

_____

7. Teaching methods used:

❑ overview   ❑ demonstration   ❑ breaking down into components

❑ visual   ❑ written   ❑ video

❑ pairs   ❑ group   ❑ individual

❑ other _____

8. Does class appeared to be well planned?   ❑ Yes   ❑ No

9. Is there an atmosphere of mutual respect?   ❑ Yes   ❑ No

10. Is class orderly and disciplined?   ❑ Yes   ❑ No

11. Is the teaching philosophy evident in class?   ❑ Yes   ❑ No

12. Are trophies and awards displayed?   ❑ Yes   ❑ No

13. If yes, do they appear to be very important?   ❑ Yes   ❑ No

14. Are resource materials available for students? ❑ Yes   ❑ No

15. Are resource materials available for parents? ❑ Yes   ❑ No

16. Does the school sponsor seminars?   ❑ Yes   ❑ No

17. Are special workshops and seminars scheduled outside of normal class
    times or do they replace regularly scheduled classes?
    ❑ Outside of Class   ❑ Replace Classes

18. When class is in progress, is there someone managing the business
(answering the phone, greeting prospective students, monitoring the
dressing rooms and lounge)?   ❑ Yes   ❑ No

19. If not, does the instructor leave class to perform these duties?

                        ❑ Yes   ❑ No

20. If the instructor leaves, does someone take over the class?

                        ❑ Yes   ❑ No

21. Are rules of the school consistently enforced?   ❑ Yes   ❑ No

22. Are students, teachers and parents having fun?   ❑ Yes   ❑ No

Additional Notes

Bibliography

Aggressive Behavior, "Examination of the Effects of Traditional and Modern Martial Arts Training on Aggressiveness," T.A. Nosanchuk and M.L. Catherine MacNeil, Carleton University, Ottawa, Ontario, Canada, 1989, Vol. 15, pages 153-159.

Anxiety in Black Belt and Nonblack-Belt Traditional Karateka, Dr. Clive Layton, Institute of Psychiatry, University of London, December 1990, Vol.71, pages 905-906.

British Journal of Medical Psychology, "Psychological research on the martial arts: An addendum to Fuller's view," Peter J. Columbus, Department of Psychology, University of Tennessee, Knoxville, Tennessee; Donadrian L. Rice, West Georgia College, Carrollton, Georgia, 1991, Vol. 64, pages 127-135.

Chart, Susan Gruskin, adapted from Illinois State Board of Education's Child Find Materials, National Institute on Early Childhood Development and Education, Office of Educational Research and Improvement, U.S. Department of Education.

Child Development, Bill Cunningham, HarperPerennial, New York, NY, 1993.

The Complete Book of Martial Arts, David Mitchell, Gallery Books, New York NY, 1989.

Comprehensive Asian Fighting Arts, Donn F. Draeger, Robert W. Smith, Kodansha International, Tokyo and New York, 1990.

Exceptional Parent, The Magazine for Families and Professionals, Parents' turn, October 1995.

How Difficult Can This Be? Understanding Learning Disabilities, The F.A.T. City Workshop, 1990, Richard D. Lavoie, M.A., M.Ed., Executive Director of the Riverview School, East Sandwich, Massachusetts,

Fitness for Youth, Jennifer Lochner, Ellie Chabi, Jill Funk, Ajit Krishnanley, Jennifer Heidmann, Dr. David Bernhardt, Dr. Bill, Bartlett, University of Wisconsin, Wis. Chapter American Academy of Pediatrics and Governor's Council on Fitness and Health, 1996.

Human Relations, "The way of the warrior: The effects of traditional martial arts training on aggression," T.A. Nosanchuk, 34:435-444.

Human Relations, "Martial Arts Training: A Novel "Cure" for Juvenile Delinquency," Michael E. Trulson, Texas A & M University, 1986, Volume 39, Number 12, pp. 1131-1140.

Journal of Sport and Exercise Psychology, 1995, Vol. 17, 294-311, "Motivational Climate, Psychological Responses, and Motor Skill Development in Children's Sport: A Field-Based Intervention Study," Marc Theeboom and Paul De Knop, Free University of Brussels, Belgium; and Maureen R. Weiss, University of Oregon, 1995, Vol. 17, pages 294-309.

Karate-Do: My Way of Life, Gichin Funakoshi, Kodansha International, Tokyo, New York and London, 1975.

N.E.W. KIDS, "Self-Defense Classes Teach More Than Technique," Lynn M. Schmidt, August 1997.

Perceptual and Motor Skills, "The Martial Arts and Mental Health: The Challenge of Managing Energy," Frank C. Seitz, Gregory D. Olson, Burt Locke, Randy Quam, 1990, Vol. 70, pages 459-464.

Perceptual and Motor Skills, "Aggressive Behavior as a Function of Taekwondo Ranking," Dennis L. Skelton, Indiana State University; Susan M. Berta, Indiana State University; Michael A. Glynn, Danville School Corporation, 1991, Vol. 72, pages 179-182.

Perceptual and Motor Skills, "Blocking and Countering in Traditional Shotokan Karate Kata," Clive Layton, Institute of Psychiatry, University of London, 1993, Vol. 76, pages 641-642.

Perceptual and Motor Skills, "Does Brief Aikido Training Reduce Aggression in Youth?", Jorge Delva-Tauilili, University of Hawaii, 1995, Vol. 80, pages 297-298.

Psychiatric Annals, Morgan, W.P., "Anxiety reduction following acute physical activity," 1979, 9, 36-45

Psychology Today, "That Mild-Mannered Bruce Lee," Michael E. Trulson, Texas A & M University, and Ghong W. Kim and Vernon R. Padgett, Marshall University, January 1985, page 79.

The Original Martial Arts Encyclopedia: Tradition-History-Pioneers, John Corcoran and Emil Farkas with Stuart Sobel, Pro-Action Publishing, Los Angeles, 1993.

Taekwon-Do, General Choi Hong Hi, 1991, International Taekwon-Do Federation, USSR.

Taekwondo Reporter, "Attention Deficit Disorder What is it? How Can It Be Treated?" Michael Kerrigan, June 1996.

Taekwondo Reporter, "Learning Disabilities & Taekwondo" Ernie and Ginny Lopez, June 1996.

Teaching Martial Arts: The Way of the Master, Sang H. Kim, Ph.D., Turtle Press, 1997.

Tonfa: Karate Weapon of Self-Defense, Fumio Demura, Ohara Publications, Inc., Santa Clarita, Calif., 1991

Your Four-Year Old; Wild and Wonderful, Louise Bates Ames, Delacorte Press, New York, NY, 1976.

Your Six-Year Old; Loving and Defiant, Louise Bates Ames and Frances L. Ilg M.D., Gesell Institute of Child Development, Delacorte Press, New York, NY, 1979.

Your Seven-Year; Life in a Minor Key, Louise Bates Ames and Carol Chase Haber, Delacorte Press, New York, NY, 1985.

Your Eight-Year; Old Lively and Outgoing, Louise Bates Ames and Carol Chase Haber, Delacorte Press, New York, NY, 1989.

Your Ten-to Fourteen-Year Old, Louise Bates Ames Ph.D., Frances L. Ilg M.D., and Sidney M. Baker M.D., Gesell Institute of Human Development, Delacorte Press, New York, NY, 1988.

Index

About the Authors

As parents of young martial artists, black belts Debra Fritsch and Ruth Hunter have experienced many of the initial questions and concerns about the martial arts.

Debra and her two daughters joined a summer program. Later, her husband enrolled, making it a rewarding family activity. Ruth's family members joined one at a time until the entire family were working out together - in the school or at home in the kitchen and backyard.

Over the years, it became evident that joining the martial arts was a positive influence on both families. Besides creating a common ground for parents and children, the martial arts developed in each participant a strong sense of personal confidence, a healthy respect for self and others, and a love of the martial arts.

The goal of this book is to give parents enough information to find a school that fits their's and their children's needs and to hopefully create a fulfilling experience for them and their families.